THE INVESTOR'S GUIDE TO EMERGING MARKETS

THE
INVESTOR'S GUIDE
TO EMERGING
MARKETS

MARK MOBIUS

IRWIN
Professional Publishing
Burr Ridge, Illinois
New York, New York

British Library Cataloging in Publication Data
A CIP catalog record for this book can be obtained from the British Library

© RICHARD D. IRWIN, INC., 1995

Originally published by Pitman Publishing, a division of Longman U.K. Ltd., copyright
1992.

This edition of *The Investor's Guide to Emerging Markets* is published by arrangement with
Pitman Publishing, London. The *Financial Times* and *FT* are trademarks of the Financial
Times, Ltd, London.

Senior sponsoring editor:	Amy Hollands Gaber
Project editor:	Karen M. Smith
Production manager:	Pat Frederickson
Interior designer:	Mercedes Santos
Compositor:	Northern Phototypesetting Co. Ltd.
Typeface:	11/13 Palatino
Printer:	Quebecor/Kingsport

Library of Congress Cataloging-in-Publication Data

Mobius, Mark.
    The investor's guide to emerging markets / Mark Mobius.
      p. cm.
    Originally pub. by Pitman Pub., c1992
    "Financial times."
    ISBN 0-7863-0320-4
    1. Investments, Foreign—Developing countries. I. Financial
times (London, England) II. Title.
HG5993.M63   1995
332.6'73'091724—dc20   94–21310

Printed in the United States of America
1 2 3 4 5 6 7 8 9 0 QK 10 9 8 7 6 5 4

Preface

This book is designed to introduce investors to the exciting and rewarding realm of emerging markets. I hope that both laypeople and professionals find the subject of interest. For the layperson, the book gives an introduction to one of the most interesting investment arenas in the world today. For the professional, it gives an insight into how one emerging markets investment manager (myself) views these markets and the philosophy he or she applies when investing in such markets.

The book is organized into eight chapters, including the definition of emerging markets, trends in emerging markets, what opportunities may be found in those markets, what investment instruments may be used, technical aspects, risks, investment strategies and techniques, and, finally, what I believe to be the future of emerging markets. As much as possible, I have tried to give a comprehensive view, but the rapid changes taking place today in the developing world make almost each sentence obsolete the day it is written.

Chapter One explains how emerging markets may be defined. That explanation encompasses the background and history of the emerging markets concept and the many antecedents to that concept starting in the 1800s when Scottish investors were investing in the *emerging market* of America. Coining the name *emerging market* had to wait until the World Bank's International Finance Corporation instituted programs aimed at encouraging capital market growth in the less developed nations of the world. Since that time there have been many "emerging markets" definitions based on a number of variables: per capita income, capital market size, development of capital market facilities and regulations, degree of restrictions on foreign investment, convertibility of the country's currency, degree of industrialization, market turnover, number of listings, and so on.

Emerging stock markets represent a small percentage of the developed countries' stock market capitalization. However, the emerging stock markets are growing dramatically faster than the developed markets. This difference in size and disparity of growth rates can also be observed in the difference in size and growth of trading volumes. In addition, concentration of market capitalization in a smaller list of companies is more prevalent in emerging markets as compared to developed markets.

Chapter Two deals with major trends in emerging markets which are causing them to become particularly rewarding investment areas. These trends include demographic changes impacting educational levels which in turn lead to higher productivity. Lower death rates, lower fertility rates, and lengthening life spans have resulted in increased educational and experience levels. In addition, there have been technological changes, which have helped emerging countries achieve higher economic growth and at a faster pace. Finally, there have been changes in economic philosophy away from reliance on Socialist, Communist, or command economy models toward market-oriented solutions.

The overwhelming reality is the great imbalance in the distribution of the world's wealth when related to area and population. While the emerging nations cover 77 percent of the world's land area and represent 85 percent of the world's population, only 23 percent of the world's gross domestic product is in those emerging nations. The underlying global trends such as the greater availability of food resulting from advances in agriculture and new progress in medicine combined with better health care in the developing nations is resulting in significant declines in death rates and extended life spans. This is leading to a narrowing of the wealth imbalance as emerging nations with their faster economic growth rates move toward the developed countries in terms of per capita wealth.

Chapter Three answers this question: Why emerging markets? Succinctly put, the reasons are: higher returns and lower volatility. Since, in the long term, stock markets reflect the underlying health and development of the economies they represent, the faster growth of the emerging nations is resulting in higher investor returns in those markets. The faster rising prices of emerging market stocks in real terms has not only been a reflection of higher economic growth in those countries, but also because of rapidly growing capital and stock markets, since the demand for financial services is accelerating as the economies grow and develop. Although the current market capitalization of emerging markets constitutes a small part of the current total global market capitalization, growth of the emerging markets capitalization has been more than double that of the developed markets. In addition, the number of new companies listed on emerging market stock exchanges is growing faster than in the developed nations. More importantly, the potential for growth is particularly high. Whereas developed countries' ratio of market capitalization to GDP averages over 80 percent, the average for emerging markets is only 33 percent with over half the emerging markets falling below 20 percent.

A number of other factors is impacting on emerging stock markets. Privatization of government enterprises is resulting in many more stock market listings. The global privatization movement is creating changes in how pension systems in emerging markets are operated. Heretofore such social security and pension schemes most often did not participate in domestic equity market investing. However, ongoing changes in the regulation of those schemes will result in more money flowing into their home country emerging stock markets. Added to this is the return of substantial sums of domestic flight capital, attracted by relaxed foreign exchange regimes and reduced government surveillance and control. Finally the growth of foreign equity investing from the United States, Japan, and Europe is creating more demand for emerging stock market shares.

Chapter Four suggests ways in which emerging market investments may be made, for example, direct investment in stock of emerging markets, indirect investment by purchasing emerging market stocks listed in developed markets, open- or closed-end mutual funds, or depository receipts of emerging market companies. The most rewarding but most difficult investment path is purchasing stocks directly in emerging stock markets. Results of individual investments have been spectacular, but for the investors without the time and resources to investigate such markets, the risks are very high. Investing through funds, however, presents an opportunity for the investor to obtain diversification, professional fund management, lower operational costs, and convenience. The history of fund organizations investing in developing countries is long and the number of such funds currently in existence is growing.

Closed-end funds or investment trusts as compared to open-end funds or unit trusts have differing advantages and disadvantages. There have been a growing number of emerging market securities listed on developed country stock exchanges. In addition the number of depository receipts such as American Depository Receipts (ADRs), Global Depository Receipts (GDRs), and International Depository Receipts (IDRs) issued by emerging country companies is growing.

Chapter Five deals with the technical aspects of emerging markets as the stock exchange characteristics, settlement and trading systems, and custody requirements. Many emerging nation stock markets started as exclusive clubs for the wealthy few and have now been expanded to cover a wide audience. However, the old structures and customs have often not met the new and expanded requirements, with disastrous results. The trend is toward more computerization and higher efficiency enabling greater turnover and faster execution. However, resistance against change and reform runs deep. Many emerging markets have the advantage of starting out new and thus are able to install the most advanced systems.

Settlement and trading systems represent a major bottleneck in the global securities business. Despite recommendations by prestigious international groups such as the "Group of Thirty," adoption of recommendations designed to remedy deficiencies have been slow in coming. Stock exchanges should strive to meet the "FELT" requirements, that is, to have market systems that are Fair, Efficient, Liquid, and Transparent. Only by having computerized trading and central registration will clearing and depository operations be able to meet the FELT requirements.

Chapter Six deals with the emerging market investing risks, including political, currency, company or investment, broker, settlement, safekeeping, and operational risks. The most important political risks are those that lead to confiscation of the investors' assets or changes in regulations or laws, which prohibit the extraction of capital and profits from the country. In addition, the lack of developed regulatory systems in developed countries presents unique and critical problems for the foreign investor. Currency risks are particularly prevalent in emerging markets because of often very high inflation and extreme currency devaluations. Also, unpredictable government measures that affect currency movements or result in barriers to currency conversion and remittance present significant risks.

Company or investment risks in emerging markets are abundant. The lack of reliable information regarding companies' background, accounts, and history is most critical. Fair and full disclosure is often not practiced in emerging stock markets, thus creating many pitfalls. Broker risks most often revolve around trading fairness and efficiency. Brokers in emerging markets are most likely to have conflicts of interest when they are taking positions in stocks their clients may be buying or selling. Also there is often an acute need for greater efficiency and lower dealing costs in emerging markets, although the developed markets are no exception to this problem. Settlement risks in emerging markets most often stem from differing settlement requirements in each market. Many of these requirements are difficult or impossible for overseas investors to meet. For example, if trades must be settled in a time frame that does not allow sufficient time for transfer of money from abroad, the foreign investors have problems. Other settlement challenges are created by the lack of uniformity in treatment of voting and dividend rights and many different classes of shares for one issuer. Safekeeping risks include a number of fraudulent activities, the most important one being counterfeit securities. Operational risks include a number of possible faults relating to the entry and exit of assets from one country to another and a host of legal and regulatory requirements. Foreign stock ownership limits, for example, present unique record-keeping and portfolio control requirements.

Chapter Seven discusses investment strategies and techniques relevant to the emerging markets. Most important is the willingness to work hard and apply strict investment discipline. Also needed is common sense, creativity, diversification, independence, or individual decision making, a willingness to take risks, an orientation toward the pursuit of value, flexibility, and a long-term view.

Research in emerging markets involves combining a global out-look and experience with a more detailed and intimate knowledge that comes from a local presence. Realistic skepticism regarding statistics and an emphasis on reliable and unbiased information sources are the cornerstones of investment research. Accounting in emerging markets requires particular scrutiny and careful study because of varying accounting methods. The more common differences in accounting systems include the treatment of taxes, off-balance-sheet items, intangibles, reserves, currency exchange, valuation of assets or inventory, depreciation, revenue recogni-tion, consolidation of subsidiaries, multiple classes of shares, inflation accounting, and loss recognition.

Chapter Eight discusses the future of emerging markets. Emerging stock markets represent one of the keys to the develop-ment of market economies and are thus a vital element necessary for improvements in the lives of people living in the less developed areas of the world. I hope this book makes some contribution toward the study of the emerging markets' phenomena. However, this study can only be a small start toward understanding the dynamic development in this field.

Fortunately, there are many emerging market investment par-ticipants each contributing knowledge and experience to the field. Professionals such as Antoine Van Agtmael and David Gill were among the original team at the International Finance Corporation who formulated many of the concepts, which nudged the emerging nations toward capital market development. Barton Biggs and his associate Madhav Dhar at Morgan Stanley have done much to foster acceptance of emerging markets investing, particu-larly among institutional investors all over the world. At Capital International, David Fisher launched the first major privately placed emerging markets fund. As one of the original global investors, Sir John Templeton led the way for U.S. global investors by venturing into the emerging market of Japan in the 1960s. Tom Hansberger at the Templeton organization conceived of the viability of a widely distributed stock exchange listed emerging markets funds in the United States and the United Kingdom. The Franklin/Templeton Group, under the able leadership of Charlie Johnson, has expanded the scope of emerging markets funds from the listed Templeton Emerging Markets Fund, Inc., in New York and the Templeton Emerging Markets Investment Trust Plc in the United Kingdom in addition to the open-ended Templeton Developing Markets Trust. Since that time there have been numerous other offerings of emerging markets funds and growing interest in such investments with benefits accruing to both investors and the world's emerging market countries.

Mark Mobius

Contents

Chapter One

Defining Emerging Markets

INTRODUCTION

T he step from international investing by fund managers to the creation of a specific emerging markets investment category has actually evolved over a long period of time and reflects the interesting evolution of global investing in general. When, in the 1800s, diligent and creative Scottish investors were purchasing farmland in the American West, they probably did not consider it any less risky than investing on the European continent. In fact, the conception was probably more oriented toward the great wealth appreciation opportunities awaiting them. The 100th anniversary report of the Alliance Trust of the United Kingdom, established in 1888, relates how that trust invested in, what was then, a primitive and emerging market—America.

The actual birth of the *emerging market* portfolio investment category had to wait until 1986 when the International Finance Corporation, the World Bank subsidiary, started to make efforts to promote capital market development in the less developed countries. During the tenure of Robert McNamara as president of the World Bank, that capital market development began to be taken seriously. This was after a great deal of groundwork was done on the theoretical foundation by economists such as Raymond Goldsmith of Yale University, who wrote about the relationships between real growth and financial intermediation. Robert McNamara initiated the establishment of a unit in the International Finance Corporation in 1971 to be a focal point for capital market development for the World Bank Group. This Group focused the attention of World Bank member countries on

1

the importance of security markets as a means of mobilizing domestic savings, and attracting foreign portfolio capital as a means of allocating savings to its most productive uses in a competitive market system.

In 1986, at the request of the World Bank's International Finance Corporation, 11 institutional investors put $50 million into an emerging markets fund. At that time, the fund manager was reported to have told investors that it might take the company one year to invest that money. As of 1993 that fund had grown to over $1 billion, and the fund managers were quoted as saying that if they were given $50 million now, it would take them a month to invest it.

In 1987 when the Templeton organization started the Templeton Emerging Markets Fund, it was the world's first such fund listed on a stock exchange with investments in emerging markets as its specific objective. The high returns of that fund, along with the success of other such funds, inspired a considerable amount of excitement in the investment world. The amounts of money pouring into emerging markets funds became significant. With the subsequent development of formal securities markets, equity legal structures, and trading systems, international equity portfolio investing became more identified with investing in those emerging areas of the world.

However, the purview of international portfolio investors was quite limited in the early days of global portfolio investing, so that when foreign investors started investing in Japan in the 1960s, it was considered to be a risky and pioneering adventure. In fact, if the concept of "emerging market" was current at that time, Japan would probably have been placed in that category. It was known as a land of inexpensive and shoddy exports, weak currency, and an unstable political future. Investors at that time were able to select Japanese stocks with price earnings ratios of 4 times—a far cry from the average 60 times that Japan's stocks reached in the 1980s.

EMERGING MARKETS: A DEFINITION

The term *emerging market*, as used in reference to stock markets, was apparently first coined by officers at the World Bank's International Finance Corporation when they began working on the concept of country funds and capital market development in the less developed regions of the world. When the Templeton organization asked me to manage the Templeton Emerging Markets Fund in 1987, a universally accepted operational definition of an emerging market did not exist. Intuitively we knew that emerging implied "developing" or "underdeveloped" but we could not ascertain what the cutting-off point for emerging versus emerged markets would be. However, the World Bank's classification of high-, middle-, and low-income countries was a good start. The low- and middle-income countries based on per capita income on that list fit our intuitive definition of what were emerging markets. Since 1987, when that original list was compiled from World Bank data, there have been a number of changes in the per capita income rankings of countries with some countries falling out of the low- and middle-income categories and others moving down from the high-income category.

The matter of oil-rich countries in the developing world had to be addressed. Although such countries as Kuwait and Saudi Arabia had per capita incomes clearly higher than the low- and middle-income countries, the distribution of that income was such that general living standards had not reached developed country status. Also, they were not fully developed in the sense that their economies were not industrialized and did not have the infrastructure or capital market system normally associated with the *developed* or industrialized world.

Since the original list was compiled there has been a dissolution of the Soviet Union and a breakaway of Eastern European countries from the Soviet empire. This has resulted in more possible entries to our list of emerging markets. We thus now have a list of 123 countries (Table 1–1) which we would consider emerging either because they (1) have low or middle per capita incomes; (2) have undeveloped capital markets so that, for example, the market capitalization of their stock markets represents a small portion of their gross national product; or (3) are not industrialized. Throughout this book these are the countries we will refer to as *developing*, *underdeveloped*, or *emerging*.

These 123 countries represent a population of over 4,443 million people and cover an area of more than 39 million square miles. The developed countries are often referred to as the industrialized countries or industrial market economies. There are 19 such countries representing a population of about 778 million and a land area about 11 million square miles (Table 1–2).

At first glance it may seem that the range of countries in which an emerging markets specialist may invest is very wide. In fact, the range of opportunities, although expanding, is quite limited for a number of reasons. First, many of the emerging countries now do not have stock markets or even any kind of formal capital market where investment may be made in an orderly and relatively safe manner. The entire organization of capital markets, in general, and stock markets, in particular, require a complex infrastructure of settlement procedures, payment systems, custodial or safekeeping facilities, regulations, and a broad range of relationships which are missing in most emerging markets today. In fact, one of the defining characteristics of an emerging market is the scarcity of such facilities.

Second, many countries forbid or restrict foreign investment or impose foreign exchange restrictions, which make it impossible to transfer money into or, most importantly, out of the country. Finally, some countries impose harsh taxation on foreign investors which make such investment unrealistic. Therefore, out of the 123 emerging countries, at the time of writing, only 24 had actively functioning stock markets in which foreigners could realistically make portfolio investments. Even among that list there were countries such as India, Korea, Taiwan, and Chile, which, although open to foreign portfolio investors, placed severe restrictions on the entry and exit of foreign investment capital.

ALTERNATIVE DEFINITIONS

Various alternative definitions have been offered for emerging markets. Some investors have defined an emerging stock market as one that represents less than a certain percentage of all the world's stock market capitalization. For example, in one case, an emerging market was defined as a market which represents less than 3 percent of the world's stock market capitalization. Some emerging market experts have eliminated certain emerging markets because they either have low security turnover or have very few companies listed. In another case, an analyst included

TABLE 1–1
Emerging countries, 1990

Country	Population (millions)	Area (in thousands) Sq.Miles	Sq.Km	GNP per Capita
China	1,134	3,696	9,561	370
India	850	1,223	3,288	350
Indonesia	178	741	1,905	570
Brazil	150	3,287	8,513	2,680
Russia	148	6,593	17,075	6,805
Nigeria	116	357	924	290
Pakistan	112	340	796	380
Bangladesh	107	507	144	210
Mexico	86	756	1,958	2,490
Vietnam	66	127	330	215
Philippines	62	116	300	730
Turkey	56	301	779	1,630
Thailand	56	198	513	1,420
Iran	56	632	1,648	2,490
Egypt	52	385	1,001	600
Ukraine	52	233	604	5,085
Ethiopia	51	438	1,222	120
Korea, South	43	38	99	5,400
Myanmar	42	261	677	280
Poland	38	121	313	1,690
Zaire	37	905	2,345	220
South Africa	36	473	1,221	2,530
Colombia	32	441	1,139	1,260
Argentina	32	1,074	2,767	2,370
Algeria	25	920	2,382	2,060
Morocco	25	177	477	950
Tanzania	25	364	945	110
Sudan, The	25	967	2,506	340
Kenya	24	225	580	370
Yugoslavia	24	39	256	3,060
Romania	23	92	238	1,640
Peru	22	496	1,285	1,160
Uzbekistan	21	173	448	2,724
Venezuela	20	352	912	2,560
Nepal	19	57	141	170
Iraq	19	168	438	1,940
Malaysia	18	128	330	2,320
Afghanistan	17	252	652	200
Sri Lanka	17	25	66	470
Kazakhstan	17	1,049	2,717	4,595
Czechoslovakia	16	30	128	3,140
Uganda	16	93	238	220
Mozambique	16	314	802	80

TABLE 1–1 (*continued*)

Country	Population (millions)	Area (in thousands) Sq.Miles	Sq.Km	GNP per Capita
Ghana	15	92	239	390
Saudi Arabia	15	865	2,150	7,050
Chile	13	292	757	1,940
Syria	13	71	185	1,000
Cameroon	12	184	475	960
Côte d'Ivoire	12	125	322	750
Madagascar	12	227	587	230
Hungary	11	36	93	2,780
Yemen	11	205	528	820
Portugal	10	36	92	4,900
Angola	10	481	1,247	600
Ecuador	10	105	284	980
Greece	10	51	132	5,990
Zimbabwe	10	151	391	640
Belarus	10	80	208	6,718
Guatemala	9	42	109	900
Bulgaria	9	43	112	5,300
Malaŵi	9	46	118	200
Mali	9	482	1,240	270
Burkina Faso	9	106	274	330
Cambodia	9	70	181	130
Niger	8	497	1,267	310
Somalia	8	246	638	120
Zambia	8	291	753	420
Tunisia	8	63	164	1,440
Rwanda	7	10	26	310
Haiti	7	11	28	370
Senegal	7	76	197	710
Bolivia	7	424	1,099	630
Azerbaijan	7	33	87	3,594
Dominican Republic	7	18	49	830
Georgia	6	27	70	3,486
Guinea	6	95	246	440
Chad	6	496	1,285	190
Hong Kong	6	−1	1	11,490
Tajikistan	5	55	143	2,206
El Salvador	5	8	21	1,110
Israel	5	8	21	10,920
Libya	5	678	1,760	5,410
Benin	5	44	113	360
Burundi	5	11	28	210
Honduras	5	43	112	590

TABLE 1–1 (*concluded*)

Country	Population (millions)	Area (in thousands)		GNP per Capita
		Sq.Miles	Sq.Km	
Laos	4	91	237	200
Togo	4	22	57	410
Sierra Leone	4	28	72	240
Paraguay	4	157	407	1,110
Papua New Guinea	4	179	463	860
Nicaragua	4	51	130	470
Lithuania	4	25	65	5,245
Moldova	4	13	34	4,829
Turkmenistan	4	189	488	3,183
Kyrgyzstan	4	77	199	3,232
Latvia	3	25	66	7,522
Armenia	3	12	30	4,490
Albania	3	11	29	1,200
Panama	3	29	77	1,830
Jamaica	3	4	11	1,500
Singapore	3	−1	−1	11,160
Costa Rica	3	20	51	1,900
Uruguay	3	68	177	2,560
Liberia	3	38	111	395
Central African Republic	3	240	623	390
Jordan	3	34	89	1,240
Lebanon	3	4	10	700
Oman	2	118	212	6,006
Lesotho	2	12	30	530
Congo	2	132	342	1,010
Kuwait	2	7	18	10,500
Mongolia	2	605	1,565	532
Mauritania	2	398	1,026	500
Namibia	2	318	824	1,245
Estonia	2	17	48	7,426
United Arab Emirates	2	30	84	19,860
Solvenia	1	8	20	10,450
Mauritius	1	−1	2	2,250
Botswana	1	225	582	2,040
Gabon	1	103	268	3,330
Trinidad and Tobago	1	2	5	3,610
Bhutan	1	18	47	190
Bahrain	1	−1	−1	7,550
Total	4,443	38,949	101,583	

Sources: World Bank, *World Development Report*; World Bank, *World Economic Outlook*, May 1992; Pan Books Ltd., *World Almanac 1993*.

TABLE 1–2
Developed Countries, 1990

Country	Population (millions)	Area (in thousands) Sq.Miles	Sq.Km	GNP per Capita (US$)
United States	250	3,679	9,373	21,790
Japan	124	146	378	25,430
Germany	80	138	357	22,320
Italy	58	116	301	16,830
United Kingdom	57	94	245	16,100
France	56	210	552	19,490
Spain	39	195	505	11,020
Canada	27	3,850	9,976	20,470
Australia	17	2,966	7,687	17,000
Netherlands, The	15	16	37	17,320
Belgium	10	12	31	15,540
Sweden	9	174	450	23,660
Austria	8	32	84	19,060
Switzerland	7	16	41	32,680
Finland	5	131	338	26,040
Denmark	5	17	43	22,080
Norway	4	125	324	23,120
Ireland	4	27	70	9,550
New Zealand	3	104	269	12,680
Total	778	9,918	31,061	

Sources: World Bank, *World Development Report*; World Bank, *World Economic Outlook*, May 1992; Pan Books Ltd., *World Almanac 1993*.

only those markets which had at least $2 billion in market turnover and 100 or more listed companies.

Some of the emerging country stock markets are very well developed and are considered by some international investors as not belonging to the emerging category. For example, Hong Kong is considered by some international investors as one of the world's major stock markets and therefore should not be included in the emerging markets list. One pension fund manager said: "I don't consider Hong Kong an emerging market because it's easy to invest there and it's very liquid." However, when one considers the income per capita of the Hong Kong population, and the fact that by 1997 it will be part of China, it is clearly in the emerging country category.

TABLE 1–3
EAFE Countries

Australia	Japan
Austria	Malaysia
Belgium	Netherlands, The
Denmark	New Zealand
Finland	Norway
France	Singapore
Germany	Spain
Hong Kong	Sweden
Irish Republic	Switzerland
Italy	United Kingdom

Some market analysts define emerging markets as any market which is not part of North America (the United States and Canada) or the EAFE (Europe, Australia, and Far East) provided that:

- There is a functional stock exchange or an active over-the-counter market.
- Securities are available to foreign portfolio investors.
- The currency is convertible or capital and income can be repatriated freely.

There are 20 EAFE markets (countries), as shown in Table 1–3. Note that the three EAFE markets most often considered to be emerging markets are Hong Kong, Singapore, and Malaysia.

The permutations and combinations are numerous and a precise definition, particularly in our changing world, may never be possible. The important point to remember is that the global securities industry has not yet defined emerging markets in a universally acceptable manner, and probably never will. Everyone seems to be agreed that, generally speaking, emerging markets require more research and custodial work than normally expected in the developed markets and often imply a greater degree of perceived risk.

WIDENING THE SCOPE

When we started investing the Templeton Emerging Markets Fund in 1987, we found that many countries were excluded from initial investment possibilities because of:

- The lack of custodial services.
- Serious foreign control restrictions.
- Other foreign portfolio investor barriers to market entry.

We therefore enlarged our purview to include investments in companies listed in major industrialized nations' stock markets that had over 50 percent of their sales, profits, or assets in the emerging nations. This provided us with the opportunity to invest indirectly in some emerging market countries which at that time restricted foreign portfolio investment. For example, on the London Stock Exchange, there were a number of companies whose operations were primarily in Africa, and one excellent company whose operations were primarily in Chile, a market that restricted foreign investment. On the New York Stock Exchange, there were also some Israeli companies. Thus, when identifying the entire scope of emerging market investments, companies eligible for investment and not just country venue must be considered, including some companies listed on major markets, such as New York or London, which have most of their assets or earnings in an emerging country, especially where direct local stock market investment may not be possible.

The emerging markets list will be transformed as economic and political situations change around the globe. In 1987, it included all countries in South and Central America; all countries in Asia, except Japan, Australia, and New Zealand; all countries in Africa; and some countries in Southern Europe, specifically Portugal, Greece, and Turkey. However, by 1992 it included all the East European countries and countries that were previously part of the USSR in addition to Russia, Ukraine, and other parts of the former Soviet empire.

Another question not yet adequately answered is: When does a stock market cease to become an emerging market? As emerging country income levels rise, and emerging stock markets become more developed and easily accessible to all international investors, we will then face the challenge of deciding which countries or markets should be deleted from the list and which should be added. Maybe there is a United Kingdom or United States emerging market in our future!

The recent term *emerging markets* may be a euphemism, but it is also a declaration of hope and faith on the part of those of us who specialize in the study of emerging stock markets. Many believe that although some of the stock markets of the developing nations may sometimes seem to be submerged, they are generally emerging into better and bigger things. Thus the term *emerging* is perhaps the best description of what we are witnessing.

EMERGING MARKET CHARACTERISTICS

According to one analyst, as of 1970 about 32 emerging countries had securities markets or stock exchanges, but only a few were fully or actively functioning. By 1992 the number of countries with functioning stock exchanges had risen to over 50. However, as at the beginning of 1992, the number of markets investable by foreigners numbered only 24.

In December 1980, those 24 main investable emerging markets had a combined market capitalization of only $144.9 billion, or less than 5 percent of all world markets and 7 percent of the Japanese, the UK, and the U.S. markets combined. As of December 1992, their market capitalization had increased to $981 billion or more than 13 percent of the market capitalization of those three developed markets (Table 1–4).

Average daily trading volume for the 24 emerging markets was $212 million in 1990 or only 8 percent of the $2,757 million traded daily in the developed countries. By 1992, daily average trading value had risen to $2,186 million in emerging markets, an increase of 931 percent compared to the three major developed markets whose daily trading volume increased by 328 percent to $11,804 million. In that year, emerging markets trading volume was thus 18 percent of the three major developed markets. (Table 1–5).

The concentration of capitalization in the emerging markets varies considerably. As of the end of 1992, for example, in Colombia, 79 percent of that market's capitalization was repre-

TABLE 1–4

*Market capitalization: Major Emerging and Developed Markets —1980
and 1992 ($ million)*

Emerging Countries	1980	1992	% Change
Hong Kong	$ 39,104	$ 171,984	+340
Mexico	12,994	139,061	+970
Korea	3,829	107,448	+2,706
Taiwan (Republic of China)	6,082	101,124	+1,563
Malaysia	12,395	94,004	+658
India	7,585	65,119	+759
Thailand	1,206	58,259	+4,731
Singapore	24,418	48,934	+100
Brazil	9,160	45,261	+394
Chile	9,400	29,644	+215
Argentina	3,864	18,633	+382
China	–	18,300	–
Philippines	3,478	13,794	+297
Indonesia	63	12,038	+19,008
Turkey	477	9,931	+1,982
Greece	3,016	9,489	+215
Portugal	191	9,213	+4,724
Pakistan	643	8,028	+1,149
Venezuela	2,657	7,600	+186
Colombia	1,605	5,681	+254
Jordan	1,605	3,365	+110
Peru	685	2,630	+284
Sri Lanka	365	1,439	+294
Bangladesh	27	316	+1,070
Total	$ 144,849	$ 981,295	+577
Developed Countries			
United States	$ 1,448,120	$ 4,023,000	+178
Japan	379,679	2,332,000	+514
United Kingdom	205,200	915,000	+346
Total	$ 2,032,999	$ 7,270,000	+258

Sources: International Finance Corporation (IFC); Swiss Bank Corporation (SBC);
Fédération Internationale des Bourses de Valeurs (FIBV); and author's estimates.

sented by the 10 largest stocks. The 10 largest capitalized stocks in
Argentina, Venezuela, Chile, and the Philippines all accounted for
50 percent or greater of total capitalization. However, in Brazil,
Pakistan, Thailand, and India, the percentage of capitalization
represented by the 10 largest capitalized stocks was less than

TABLE 1–5

Average Daily Trading Volume: Major Emerging and Developed Markets—Estimated ($ million)

Emerging Countries	1980	1992	% Change
Korea	$ 8.50	$ 597.26	+6,927
Hong Kong	87.39	362.80	+315
Taiwan	20.47	352.78	+1,624
Thailand	1.40	183.59	+13,014
Mexico	14.83	162.60	+997
Malaysia	11.69	119.55	+923
Singapore	16.60	71.30	+330
Brazil	24.15	71.52	+196
Argentina	4.95	65.30	+1,219
Portugal	0.01	32.73	+327,200
India	12.55	28.51	+127
Turkey	0.05	25.33	+50,560
China (Shenzhen)	n/a	25.07	n/a
China (Shanghai)	n/a	20.30	n/a
Indonesia	0.04	16.29	+40,625
Philippines	2.81	12.49	+344
Greece	0.39	8.85	+2,169
Chile	2.49	6.91	+177
Jordan	0.63	6.83	+984
Venezuela	0.27	6.65	+2,363
Pakistan	0.82	5.25	+540
Colombia	0.85	1.92	+126
Peru	0.61	1.78	+192
Sri Lanka	0.01	0.46	+4,500
Bangladesh	0.002	0.04	+1,900
Total	$ 212	$ 2,186	+931
Developed Countries	1980	1992	% Change
United States	1,862.80	6,899.01	+270
United Kingdom	162.69	3,023.00	+1,758
Japan	731.50	1,882.32	+157
Total	2,756.99	11,804.33	+328

Note: Turkey—1983; Bangladesh and Pakistan—1984; and Sri Lanka—1985.

Sources: International Finance Corporation (IFC) and National Research Institute (NRI).

30 percent (Table 1–6). By comparison, in Japan, the United States, and United Kingdom, the concentration in 1992 was between 15 percent and 24 percent.

The concentration of trading value is even more varied than the market capitalization concentration due to the tendency of many emerging market companies to be closely held by families or governments with the number of shares available for trading or purchase (the "free float") limited. For example, in Venezuela, Argentina, Colombia, Indonesia, Chile, Brazil, and Greece, 50 percent or more of the 1992 trading value was concentrated in 10 stocks. However, in the case of Pakistan, Taiwan, Malaysia, and Turkey, the concentration of trading in the 10 most active stocks was less than 20 percent (Table 1–7). By comparison, during 1992 in the United Kingdom, the 10 most active stocks represented 18 percent of total trading volume while in the United States it was 7 percent and in Japan 6 percent.

As with the developed markets, emerging markets often have more than one stock exchange. In 1991–92, an estimated 34 emerging countries had at least 38 stock exchanges between them, with a total of 11,864 companies listed and market capitalization of approximately $1,174 billion (Table 1–8). At that time, there were a total of 32 stock exchanges in 19 developed countries with 26,206 companies listed representing a market capitalization of $14,794 billion (Table 1–9). I say 'at least' because in some countries such as India, there are more exchanges for which complete and accurate data are not available. India has, for example, over 10 active stock exchanges, many trading the same stocks in addition to shares unique to their region.

TABLE 1–6

Capitalization Concentration: Leading Emerging and Developed Markets,
1992

	Share of Market Capitalization Held by 10 Largest Stocks
Emerging Countries	
Colombia	79
Argentina	69
Venezuela	60
Chile	54
Philippines	52
Jordan	49
Greece	44
Turkey	40
Indonesia	39
Mexico	32
Malaysia	31
Portugal	31
Korea	31
Taiwan (Republic of China)	30
Brazil	29
Thailand	29
Pakistan	23
India	23
Average	41
Developed Countries	
United Kingdom	24
Japan	17
United States	15
Average	19

Sources: International Finance Corporation and author's estimates.

TABLE 1–7
Trading Value Concentration: Leading Emerging and Developed Markets

	Share of Value Traded Held by 10 Most Active Stocks
Emerging Countries	
Venezuela	80
Argentina	73
Colombia	63
Indonesia	61
Chile	58
Brazil	51
Greece	50
Mexico	39
Thailand	36
India	32
Jordan	32
Philippines	31
Portugal	22
Korea	22
Pakistan	19
Taiwan	15
Malaysia	14
Turkey	11
Average	39
Developed Countries	
United Kingdom	18
United States	7
Japan	6
Average	10

Sources: International Finance Corporation; *Datastream;* and author's estimates.

TABLE 1–8
Emerging Markets Stock Exchanges, 1991–1992

Exchange	Country	Number of Listed Companies	Market Capitalization ($million)
Buenos Aires	Argentina	175	$ 18,633
Dhākā	Bangladesh	145	316
São Paulo	Brazil	565	45,261
Rio de Janeiro	Brazil	590	40,147
Santiago	Chile	245	29,644
Shanghai	China	29	8,900
Shenzhen	China	23	9,400
Bogotá	Colombia	80	5,681
Cairo	Egypt	573	1,835
Athens	Greece	129	9,489
Hong Kong	Hong Kong	413	171,984
Bombay	India	2,781	65,119
Madras	India	660	1,446
Jakarta	Indonesia	155	12,038
Tel-Aviv	Israel	367	12,089
Amman	Jordan	103	3,365
Nairobi	Kenya	53	460
Korea	Korea, South	688	107,448
Kuala Lumpur	Malaysia	369	94,004
Mauritius	Mauritius	19	337
Mexican	Mexico	195	139,061
Karachi	Pakistan	628	8,028
Lima	Peru	287	2,630
Makati/Manila	Philippines	170	13,794
Lisbon	Portugal	191	9,213
Oporto	Portugal	187	9,961
Colombo	Sri Lanka	190	1,439
Singapore	Singapore	213	48,934
Johannesburg	South Africa	728	123,981
Taiwan	Taiwan	256	101,124
Thailand	Thailand	312	58,259
Trinidad and Tobago	Trinidad and Tobago	29	671
Tunis	Tunisia	15	637
Istanbul	Turkey	145	9,931
Montevideo	Uruguay	26	44
Caracas	Venezuela	66	7,600
Belgrade	Yugoslavia	2	53
Zimbabwe	Zimbabwe	62	628
Total		$ 11,864	$ 1,173,584

Sources: London Stock Exchange, *Quality of Markets Review, Autumn Edition 1992*;
Euromoney; International Finance Corporation; Fédération Internationale des Bourses de
Valeurs; and author's estimates.

TABLE 1–9
Developed Markets Stock Exchanges, 1991–1992

Exchange	Country	Number of Listed Companies	Market Capitalization ($millions)
Australian	Australia	1,073	135,153
Vienna	Austria	131	19,750
Brussels	Belgium	176	64,105
Alberta	Canada	690	16,094
Vancouver	Canada	1,915	3,234
Toronto	Canada	1,138	255,265
Montreal	Canada	609	216,099
Copenhagen	Denmark	294	32,489
Helsinki	Finland	63	11,954
Paris	France	839	327,360
Germany (Federation of Exchanges)	Germany	667	337,870
Milan	Italy	348	122,693
Nagoya	Japan	550	1,491,090
Osaka	Japan	1,163	1,955,074
Niigata	Japan	199	934,878
Tokyo	Japan	1,766	2,224,651
Luxembourg	Luxembourg	70	11,833
Amsterdam	Netherlands, The	284	170,744
New Zealand	New Zealand	139	15,324
Oslo	Norway	112	17,840
Bilbao	Spain	500	95,406
Madrid	Spain	433	116,224
Barcelona	Spain	406	92,830
Stockholm	Sweden	127	74,895
Basle	Switzerland	388	164,551
Geneva	Switzerland	1,078	171,291
Zurich	Switzerland	182	173,738
United Kingdom	United Kingdom	2,330	954,883
American (New York)	United States	860	72,795
Pacific (San Francisco)	United States	1,476	1,723
New York	United States	2,089	3,934,085
Nasdaq (New York)	United States	4,111	578,310
Total		26,206	14,794,231

Sources: London Stock Exchange, *Quality of Markets Review, Autumn Edition 1992;*
Euromoney; International Finance Corporation; Fédération Internationale des Bourses de
Valeurs; and author's estimates.

Chapter Two

Trends in Emerging Markets

CONFLUENCE OF PHILOSOPHICAL, ECONOMIC, AND DEMOGRAPHIC FACTORS

T he world of the later 20th century is being subjected to a number of philosophical, economic, and demographic trends, which have resulted in the growing importance of emerging markets and their influence on financial markets around the world. First, there is a composite of *demographic factors*, the creation of which are having an impact on education and thus wealth. Trends toward lower death rates, lower fertility rates, and lengthening life spans have had a dramatic impact on educational and experience levels, influencing economic abilities and aspirations. Second, there has been the powerful impact of *technology*, which has facilitated better communications and higher productivity, particularly in the emerging nations. Third, there has been a dramatic *change in economic philosophy*, with a growing awareness of the complexity of human economic endeavor, acknowledgment of the failure of central economic planning to raise the living standards of the world's people, and a belief that market economic systems are most successful in stimulating economic growth. These influences have resulted in such phenomena as burgeoning privatization of state-owned organizations which, in turn, have required substantially increased capital market activity. These developments have been augmented by greater world trade leading to export-led growth in the emerging markets, more manageable debt trends in emerging markets, and tax reforms.

TABLE 2-1
Number of Countries, Gross Domestic Product Area and Population, 1990

	Number of Countries	(%)	GDP ($ billion)	(%)
Developed countries	19	13	$ 16,222	77
Emerging countries	123	87	4,968	23
Total	142	100	$ 21,190	100

	Area			Population	
	Sq.Miles	Sq.Km	(%)	(million)	(%)
Developed countries	12,032	31,163	23	778	15
Emerging countries	39,221	101,583	77	4,443	85
Total	51,253	132,746	100	5,221	100

Source: World Bank.

POPULATION, NATURAL RESOURCES, AND ECONOMIC IMBALANCE

The world today is characterized by a great imbalance in the distribution of wealth. In 1990, 77 percent of the world's land area, 85 percent of the world's population, and 87 percent of all the world's governments were in the emerging countries, but only 23 percent of the world's gross domestic product (GDP) was found there. At that time, emerging countries had a total population of 4,443 million compared to only 778 million in the developed countries. Of the world's total land area, 39,221,196 square miles were in emerging countries versus 12,032,034 square miles in the developed countries. Of the total number of governments or nations, 123 were in the emerging areas and only 19 in developed areas. However, of the total world's estimated $21,190 billion gross domestic product, $16,222 billion was in the emerging countries and $4,968 billion in the developed countries (Table 2-1). This fundamental gap between population, area, and wealth is narrowing for a number of demographic, technological, and philo-

TABLE 2-2
Crude Death Rate (Per 1,000 Population)

	1960	1990	% Change, 1960–90
Developed countries	11	10	−9
Emerging countries	15	8	−47

Source: World Bank, *World Development Report 1981 to 1992.*

sophical reasons, making many of the emerging markets the fastest growing and most dynamic areas of the world.

With the larger portion of the world's land mass, the emerging nations represent at least that much in natural resources waiting for development. The unlocking of these resources as a result of liberalized investment policies will have a dramatic impact on the economic growth of many of the emerging nations. One example of how large some of these investments can be was announced in December 1992 when the giant company, Exxon, reached an agreement with the Indonesian government to develop a gas field at a cost of $17 billion. This development was reported to guarantee that Indonesia will be the world's leading exporter of liquified natural gas into the next century. It will raise the country's natural gas reserves by an estimated 45 trillion cubic feet, to more than 100 trillion cubic feet, and will include the largest offshore platforms ever built.

DEMOGRAPHIC FACTORS

There are a number of global demographic trends, which have had, and will continue to have, a dramatic impact on economic growth and the development of the emerging market world. As a result of better nutrition and better health care, people around the world, particularly in the emerging markets, are living longer, and having fewer children, while infant mortality is falling.

Crude death rate. Between 1960 and 1990, the crude death rate in 24 emerging countries fell by over 47 percent compared to a 9 percent drop for developed countries (Table 2–2).

TABLE 2–3
Infant Mortality Rate (Deaths per 1,000 Live Births in That Year)

	1960	1990	% Change, 1960–90
Developed countries	28	7	−75
Emerging countries	109	42	−61

Source: World Bank, *World Development Report 1981 to 1992.*

TABLE 2–4
Life Expectancy at Birth (Years)

	1960	1990	% Change, 1960–1990
Developed countries	70	77	+10
Emerging countries	54	68	+26

Source: *World Bank, World Development Report 1981 to 1992.*

Infant mortality.   Infant mortality rates are falling in the emerging countries about as fast as in the developed countries. Infant mortality rates between 1960 and 1990 in the emerging markets fell by over 61 percent, from 109 per 1,000 live births to 42 per 1,000, compared to a 75 percent drop in the developed countries (Table 2–3).

Life expectancy.   Life expectancy at birth has been moving up at a steady pace for the entire world, but at a faster pace in the emerging countries. Between 1960 and 1990, life expectancy in emerging countries rose by 26 percent compared to 10 percent in the developed countries (Table 2–4).

Between 1905 and 1978, life expectancy at birth for India rose from 23 years of age to 41 years of age. In the Republic of Korea (South Korea), between 1927 and 1987, life expectancy rose from 38 years of age to 50. In Guatemala, between 1950 and 1984, the World Bank estimates that life expectancy at birth rose from 44 years of age to 52.

The decline in the crude death rate and infant mortality rate has been high for the emerging countries because of the very dramatic

TABLE 2–5
Total Fertility Rate

	1965	1990	% Change, 1965–90
Developed countries	2.6	1.7	−35
Emerging countries	5.6	3.2	−43

Source: *World Bank, World Development Report 1981 to 1992.*

impact of better health care, lower cost of medicines, availability of more effective medicines, and better nutrition. In Brazil, between 1950 and 1991, the number of physicians per 1,000 people rose from an average of 0.4 to 1.5, an increase of 275 percent. In Turkey during that same period, the average rose from 0.3 to 0.8, a 166 percent change. In Greece, the number rose from 1.4 per 1,000 people to 3.1 physicians per 1,000, a 121 percent change.

While life expectancies are increasing, fertility and birth rates are declining. A United Nations' report has shown sharp drops in Third World fertility rates in the last 20 years due to significant increases in the use of contraceptives. Between 1965 and 1990, the total fertility rate of the developed countries fell by an average of 35 percent, from an average of 2.6 children that would be born to a woman if she were to live to the end of her childbearing years, to an average of 1.7 in 1990. From 1965 to 1990, emerging nations' fertility rates fell from an average of 5.6 children to 3.2, a fall of 43 percent (Table 2–5).

While the fertility rate took 25 years to fall from 2.6 to 1.7 in the developed world, the same drop took 15 years in Colombia, 8 years in Thailand, and only 7 years in Portugal. The number of married women of reproductive age in the developing world who are using contraception has risen 10 fold in the past 25 years to 380 million.

Between 1960 and 1990 the crude birthrates per 1,000 population for emerging countries fell from an average of 41 per 1,000 population to 25, a 39 percent drop. In the developed countries, the fall was from 19 to 13, a 32 percent decrease (Table 2–6).

Thus, although the fertility and birthrates of the emerging countries are falling at about or faster than the developed countries, the absolute rates in the emerging countries are still

TABLE 2–6
Crude Birth Rate (Per 1,000 Population)

	1960	1990	% Change, 1960–90
Developed countries	19	13	−32
Emerging countries	41	25	−39

Source: *World Bank, World Development Report 1981 to 1992.*

TABLE 2–7
Population (Million)

	1981	1991	% Change, 1981–91
Five major developed countries	520	567	+9
Emerging countries	2,568	3,112	+21

Sources: *World Bank, World Development Report 1981*; Pan Books Ltd., *World Almanac 1993*; and author's estimates.

high. The population growth in emerging countries is continuing to rise faster than in the developed countries. Between 1981 and 1991, the five major developed countries (France, Germany, United Kingdom, Japan, and the United States) rose in population from 520 million to 567 million, a 9 percent increase. During that same period, the population in 24 emerging nations rose from 2,568 million to 3,112 million, a 21 percent increase (Table 2–7).

Possible food shortages. The Malthusian fear that the world would be taken over by ever expanding populations, thereby creating a food shortage disaster, has not been proved by the statistics. Not so long ago, many were predicting a global food disaster caused by rising populations and static or lower food production. These predictions have simply been proved wrong. Technology has solved food scarcity demands, although the food distribution challenge remains. For example, an estimated 2.7 billion people, primarily in Asia, rely on rice as their main source of calories. Improved rice culture, through research and new breeding, has resulted in an increase in rice production in the past 25 years greater than the rapid population increase in Asia. During that time, the real price of rice has been halved and the predicted disastrous food shortage has not occurred.

The frightening prospect of urbanization with overcrowded and poor cities also may not be an accurate picture. Recent evidence indicates that population density and the percentage of urban population appears to have a favorable correlation with a nation's prospects of having faster economic growth. Certainly, as nations grow, they tend to become industrialized, and there is a tendency to become more urbanized.

LITERACY AND EDUCATION CHANGES

Strides in the creation, production, and distribution of new medicines and drugs, combined with the greater availability of food, has led to longer average life spans. People with a longer life span have more time to learn how to read, write, and develop skills. Although more than 1 billion adults are still illiterate in the developing world, the strides made in literacy growth have been phenomenal. Increased life expectancies make learning skills and experience more practical and worthwhile. The result has been dramatic improvements in adult literacy witnessed in many countries.

The Rise of Literacy

Moreover, multilateral development institutions are increasing their emphasis on education in the developing world in an effort to help raise living standards. In almost all the emerging nations, adult literacy, admittedly in some cases starting from a low base, is rising rapidly. In 1930, less than 10 percent of the Indonesian population could read, but by 1980 this proportion had risen to 60 percent. Between 1960 and 1990, literacy in China grew from 43 percent of the population to 73 percent of the adult population, an increase of 70 percent. In that same period adult literacy in India rose from 28 percent of the adult population to 48 percent, a 71 percent change. In Pakistan, between 1960 and 1990, adult literacy rose from 15 percent of all adults to 35 percent, a 133 percent rise,

TABLE 2–8
Adult Literacy (Percent)

Emerging Countries	1960	1980	1990	% Change, 1960–1990
Jordan	32	70	80	+150
Pakistan	15	24	35	+133
Turkey	38	60	81	+113
Indonesia	39	62	77	+97
India	28	36	48	+71
China	43	69	73	+70
Bangladesh	22	26	35	+59
Malaysia	53	60	78	+47
Venezuela	63	82	88	+40
Peru	61	80	85	+39
Colombia	63	81	87	+38
Thailand	68	86	93	+37
Portugal	63	78	85	+35
Mexico	65	83	87	+34
Korea	71	93	95	+34
Brazil	61	76	81	+33
Philippines	72	75	90	+25
Sri Lanka	75	85	88	+17
Argentina	91	93	95	+4
Average	54	69	78	+44

Source: *World Bank, World Development Report* 1983 and 1991.

while in Turkey during that period, the increase was 113 percent, going from 38 percent of the adult population to 81 percent. In recent times, the emerging nations have continued to improve literacy. For 19 emerging nations, between 1960 and 1990, adult literacy rose by an average of 44 percent with countries such as Jordan, Pakistan, and Turkey raising adult literacy levels by more than 100 percent. A number of countries have reached adult literacy levels of more than 90 percent, the same as the major industrialized countries (Table 2–8).

These developments parallel the change that took place in Japan and other countries as they have emerged into developed markets. Between 1850 and 1920, for example, Japan's adult literacy rose from about 10 percent to over 80 percent. Now the new emerging markets are duplicating that development, but at a faster pace because of modern innovations in communications and education.

Better health care has resulted in improvements in the ability of people to learn, because better health is directly related to people's alertness, capacity for learning, and ability to cope with life. A prolonged life span makes investments, knowledge, and skills more worthwhile. The changing role of women in the world is also having an impact. The education of women is beginning to explain important changes in infant mortality. In countries where girls lack education compared to boys, there is twice the rate of infant mortality. Healthier and educated mothers strongly influence the early physical and mental development of their children.

With a longer life, people have more time to learn how to read, write, and experience. A better educated person is able to absorb new information faster and apply unfamiliar data and new processes more effectively. Studies have found that a one-year increase in schooling can augment wages by more than 10 percent and raises GDP significantly. In Peru, for example, it was found that if farmers had an additional year of schooling, it increased their probability of adopting modern farm technology by 45 percent. In Thailand, farmers with four years of schooling were three times more likely to use new fertilizers and other chemical inputs than farmers with one to three years of school.

It is also evident that education promotes entrepreneurship. Entrepreneurs see new opportunities, are willing to take risks and change methods. They thus make the connection from innovation to actual production. These are the foundations of strong future growth, which portfolio managers seek to harness for investors. They are the signals that tell us that an economy has the potential to emerge. Someone once said: "The road to success is paved with education."

Therefore, it is clear that countries with high rates of education have a measurable bias toward higher economic growth. It is important to know, however, that more than one billion adults are still illiterate in the emerging world, but this points the way toward astounding possible growth in view of the accelerating exchange of information brought about by communications technology.

SAVINGS RATES

Savings rates in the emerging world have tended to be higher than those of the developed countries for a number of cultural and demographic reasons. The younger average age of emerging market populations means that a greater portion of the population has already entered or soon will be entering the most productive years of their lives. It is during these years that people have more money to build up their savings, thus leading to a generally higher savings rate in the emerging markets. In addition, there are cultural factors which lead to high savings rates. In China, for example, the traditions of family unity and saving for future generations have led to high savings rates. Generally in Asia, savings rates have far outpaced those of the developed nations. For example, the savings rates of the G–7 countries fell from 13 percent of GDP during the 1970 to 1980 decade, to a savings rate of 8.1 percent in 1990 and 7.8 percent in 1992. In Asia, however, an average savings rate of 13 percent of GDP has been estimated by the International Monetary Fund. This, of course, has led to higher rates of bank deposits and reserves so that an estimated 41 percent of global bank reserves are now in the seven leading east Asian economies compared to only 17 percent in 1980.

TECHNOLOGICAL CHANGE

The impact of new technologies on the ability of the people of emerging countries to learn is great. Some economists have stated that the four key elements for a country to generate a high standard of living include: (1) natural resources, (2) capital, (3) technology, and (4) a skilled workforce.

The interplay between technology and a more skilled workforce is evident. As the standard of education in emerging nations rises, the ability to absorb technology grows. For this reason, one economist said, "Talented people are a more important resource than any man-made device or corporate strategy." Emerging nations can now take advantage of the technological developments that have been produced by the developed nations over the last century, and apply the very best of this technology to their own productive growth.

Communications Revolution

Probably the biggest impact that technology has made is the growth in communication technology. Recent strides in the ability to communicate around the world less expensively and more effectively have enabled the emerging nations to obtain information and technology more rapidly. The explosive growth in telephones, television, air travel, and automobiles mean that more and more emerging nations are able to communicate with the rest of the world at a lower cost and more effectively.

In 1945, Arthur C. Clarke, the engineer and science fiction author, articulated the idea of a communication satellite. Only 12 years later, the first artificial satellite carrying a radio transmitter (Sputnik) was launched, and 17 years later, the first communication satellite (Telstar) was launched. It is interesting to note that despite his profound ability to predict technological events, Clarke could not predict the ramifications of technological development which, even in 1945, were moving faster than anyone realized. In his 1945 paper on communication satellites, he predicted that the satellites would be manned space stations, since workers would be needed to replace the various vacuum tubes in the satellite. In those days, thousands of short-life vacuum tubes were needed to operate transmitters, so it was impossible for him to believe in 1945 that TV relay stations could operate without a staff of engineers changing tubes and checking circuits. However, the transistor and the solid state revolution came along within a few years, and what he assumed would have to be done by large manned stations could then be achieved by satellites the size of oil drums.

Mass Communications

The impact of just satellite technology combined with advances in photography and surveillance has provided more information about the world than ever before. Some say that the communication satellite was largely responsible for preventing the cold war turning into a hot war by creating a more transparent world and reducing the uncertainty threshold. The spread of mass communications, particularly television, has had a dramatic impact on how people view themselves in the world. This has resulted in further opportunities for the introduction of new technology.

TABLE 2–9
Television Homes (Million)

	1980	1992	% Change, 1980–92
Developed countries	171	211	+23
Emerging countries	103	259	+151

Source: Screen Digest Ltd., *Screen Digest*.

Television is bringing new ideas to millions of emerging market populations, ideas that are having a revolutionary impact on their economic behavior. Between 1980 and 1992, the number of homes with televisions in emerging countries grew by 151 percent, compared to a 23 percent increase in developed countries (Table 2–9).

In some countries that started from a low base, the growth has been phenomenal (Table 2–10). For example, between 1980 and 1992 the number of television homes in India increased from 1.2 million to 15.8 million, an increase of 1,217 percent.

The introduction of satellite mass communication systems is not only having a dramatic impact on the transfer of technology but also on the transfer of new ideas. Observations from all over the world indicate that the penetration of television is revolutionizing how people in even the most isolated regions think and behave. The impact of viewing an American TV program on "Lifestyles of the Rich and Famous" on slum-dwellers in Bombay or boat people in China is difficult to predict.

Star TV, based in Hong Kong and Asia's largest satellite network, as of 1993 reached an estimated 12 million households throughout Asia in addition to hotels and restaurants in 38 countries from India to Israel, and from China to the Philippines. In India, the fastest growing market, the number of viewers increased almost 160 percent in nine months of 1993 alone to 3.3 million households. The system's largest audience is in China with 4.8 million households, followed by Taiwan with 1.9 million.

The availability of low-cost satellite dishes enables the establishment of small networks in even the remotest and poorest areas. In central India, for example, television shop owners install a

TABLE 2–10
Television Homes in Emerging Countries (Million)

Emerging countries	1980	1992	% Change, 1980–92
Sri Lanka	0.03	1.0	+3,233
India	1.2	15.8	+1,217
Thailand	0.8	5.3	+563
Pakistan	0.8	3.1	+288
Bangladesh	0.2	0.7	+250
Brazil	15.0	43.3	+189
China	35.0	98.4	+181
Malaysia	1.0	2.7	+170
Philippines	2.1	5.0	+138
Portugal	1.3	3.0	+131
Colombia	2.9	6.6	+128
Indonesia	9.4	21.4	+128
Venezuela	1.7	3.8	+124
Peru	0.9	1.9	+111
Turkey	3.6	6.9	+92
Korea, South	6.3	10.4	+65
Chile	2.2	3.6	+64
Mexico	6.5	10.4	+60
South Africa	2.0	3.2	+60
Singapore	0.4	0.6	+50
Jordan	0.2	0.3	+50
Hong Kong	1.1	1.5	+36
Greece	2.5	3.3	+32
Argentina	5.4	7.1	+31
Total	103	259	+152

Source: Screen Digest Ltd., *Screen Digest*.

satellite dish for about $2,400 and then obtain subscribers who pay about $3 a month to receive the satellite TV channels.

This ability to establish contact with the rest of the world is short-circuiting the information flow so that governments around the world find it more difficult to control the flow of information to their populations. One senior Chinese journalist once said, "The government has already lost control over information. The leaders may not know yet, but these days they simply can't control what people know." The information revolution in China expanded in the 1980s with the spread of shortwave radios and the end of the

TABLE 2–11
Number of Telephones (Per 1000 Population)

Emerging Countries	1960–1965	1991, Most Recent Estimate	% Change, 1960–91
Philippines	10	154	+1,440
Korea, South	40	303	+658
Turkey	25	125	+400
Malaysia	24	91	+279
Singapore	143	500	+250
Brazil	29	91	+214
Indonesia	2	6	+200
Mexico	48	132	+175
Pakistan	3	8	+167
Thailand	8	21	+163
China	4	10	+150
Greece	200	417	+109
Sri Lanka	5	10	+100
Hong Kong	250	500	+100
Bangladesh	1	2	+100
Portugal	125	238	+90
Venezuela	53	91	+72
Chile	42	67	+60
Colombia	50	77	+54
South Africa	77	118	+53
Argentina	77	111	+44
Peru	24	33	+38
Average	56	141	+152

Source: World Bank, *Social Indicators of Development, 1990*; Pan Books Ltd., *World Almanac 1993*.

ban on listening to broadcasts by the Voice of America and the British Broadcasting Corporation.

Newspaper circulation has also blossomed. Between 1950 and 1991, newspaper circulation per thousand population in emerging countries grew from 51 per thousand to 83 per thousand, a 63 percent change.

Telephonic Communications

In emerging countries, the number of telephones per thousand population increased on the average of 152 percent between 1960 and 1991. The number of telephones now available to emerging nation populations is greater than it has ever been before. Between

1960 and 1991, the number of telephones per 1,000 people in Brazil rose from 29 to 91, a 214 percent increase. In China, the increase was 150 percent, from 4 to 10 per 1,000. In Korea it was from 40 telephones to 303 telephones, a 658 percent change in the 1960 to 1991 period. The Philippines increased the number from 10 to 154 telephones per 1,000 people, a 1,440 percent increase in the 1960 to 1991 period (Table 2–11).

Because of the low density of telephones and the rise in living standards, demand for telephone services has soared. Residents in cities often wait two years and pay exorbitant fees for telephones to be installed. In China, according to one estimate, the number of applicants rises annually by about 16 percent. The government is taking steps to increase capacity and is also improving communications in remote areas, particularly those with strong national minorities such as Xinjiang, Inner Mongolia, and Tibet.

As a result of the introduction of mobile phones, emerging countries can now leapfrog into the telephonic age without suffering the high cost of laying many land lines. The establishment of cellular operators is mushrooming throughout the emerging world, creating modern reliable telephone links almost overnight. By the end of 1993, a joint venture between the state-owned Hungarian telecommunications company and US West, Inc. was expected to complete a nationwide system of mobile phones. Since starting in 1990, over 24,000 subscribers were obtained, with one-third using mobile phones as their only telephone. Such a demand has encouraged companies such as US West, Inc., to establish franchises in the Czech Republic and Slovak Republic, in Moscow, St. Petersburg, and 11 other Russian cities.

There have been a number of other strides in technology which will make wireless communication even more efficient and cost effective. The movement from analog systems to new digital technologies will mean that both cellular and landline telephone systems will be able to expand capacity dramatically, with data communications becoming more efficient. Other plans call for satellite telephone systems, which enable telephones to be linked around the globe through a system of low-orbiting satellites. Facsimile machines are proliferating throughout the emerging world so that information can be transmitted with even more efficiency.

TABLE 2–12
Periods During Which Output Per Person Doubled

Country and Period	Years
United Kingdom, 1780–1838	58
United States, 1839–86	47
Japan, 1885–1919	34
Turkey, 1857–77	20
Brazil, 1961–79	18
Republic of Korea, 1966–77	11
China, 1977–87	10

Source: World Bank, *World Development Report 1991.*

PRODUCTIVITY ADVANCES

The combination of better education, higher capital inputs, and the impact of new technology is having a dramatic and accelerating impact on productivity growth in the emerging nations. Examining periods when output per person doubled in selected countries indicates that productivity growth is accelerating in emerging nations. According to the World Bank, the United Kingdom took more than 50 years between 1780 and 1838 to double output per person. The United States did it in about 47 years, whereas Japan was able to double output per person in about 34 years. However, the emerging nations of Turkey, Brazil, Korea, and China all did it in less than 21 years, and in the case of the Republic of Korea and China, they have been able to do it in 11 years or less (Table 2–12).

In addition, the image of developing countries' workforces being not as hardworking as those in the developed markets has been contradicted. Recent studies show that not only does productivity in many of the emerging market nations equal or exceed that of the developed markets, but the working hours in developing nations, when including the informal markets, also compare well. For example, one study showed that almost one-third of economically active Brazilians worked more than 48 hours a week, putting them second only to the Japanese, and ahead of the Germans, Americans, French, English, and Canadians.

CHANGES IN ECONOMIC AND POLITICAL PHILOSOPHY

In the early 1960s, when I was studying economic development theory at the Massachusetts Institute of Technology, many of the faculty members were spending a significant portion of their talents on understanding how and why countries grew and what could be done to stimulate economic expansion in the so-called underdeveloped countries. (Incidentally, the word *underdeveloped* was soon replaced, as the economists were reminded that, to some degree, it reflected ethnocentric thinking and was not very acceptable to aid-recipient countries. We thus progressed to developing, Third World, and the South.)

Trying to understand economic development in the 1960s was a humbling experience for the economists and officials in multinational assistance organizations. The U.S. Agency for International Development spearheaded the global program to produce economic growth in the less developed nations, but the results were disappointing indeed—so much so that today the entire concept of bilateral aid without recipient country reform and structural change has been denigrated.

Since the 1960s, economic thought has come a long way, and the importance of market-oriented policies and capital market development now absorbs a great deal of attention of the multilateral institutions. It is not surprising then, that the idea of emerging markets, as applied to portfolio investing, was originated by the International Finance Corporation, a subsidiary of the World Bank.

International Aid Programs

The case against international aid programs has been well articulated by many economists and observers. According to some estimates, since World War II, subsidies in the form of grants or soft loans from the richer countries to the poorer ones have mushroomed from a few hundred million dollars a year to about $50 billion by the 1980s. The criticism is that the subsidies do not go to the poor people of these countries, but to their rulers who are often directly responsible for the bad condition of their subjects. There is also the argument that such aid has the effect of keeping bad governments in place. Even Iraq, during the time when it was enjoying huge oil revenues in the 1980s, received millions of dollars of Western aid, which allowed that country to build up a huge military arsenal. Aid has often been cited as being responsible for regional wars. One commentator has cited the cases of India and Pakistan, Iran and Iraq, Uganda and Tanzania, which were at war with each other but were receiving aid from the West.

One study has shown that since the early 1960s, African nations have collected more than $300 billion in aid. In the 1980s, Africans were receiving about 22 percent of the West's total development assistance. In one case, $9 billion was given to Tanzania between 1970 and 1988, more than four times that country's 1988 gross domestic product. Africa is littered with a number of "white elephants," including fancy airports, conference halls and new capital cities. These major projects have tended to enrich the country's leaders rather than to help the population at large. One Lesotho chief has been quoted as saying, "We have two problems: rats and government." Another African proverb states, "If you rely on somebody for food, you will go without breakfast." As billions of dollars have been siphoned off into foreign bank accounts by African rulers, it is now becoming evident that aid has not stimulated economic growth, and may have even hindered it by inhibiting the necessary economic reform and changes in political structure.

Economists are beginning to revise their thinking regarding what is necessary for economic development and change. Probably one of the most articulate proponents of structural change is Richard Rahn, who flatly states that the capitalistic system is man's greatest invention and free markets are necessary for economic development. However, he mentions a number of key elements necessary for a successful economic system:

- The innovation of double-entry bookkeeping.
- Fair taxation, which does not expropriate or exploit.
- A social ethic, which emphasizes hard work.
- The concept of private property rights, which are forcefully protected.
- The idea of a free trading system globally.
- A fair and efficient legal system.

- Low levels of government spending and therefore low taxation.
- Low regulatory burdens.

The key concept is that free markets provide for free prices, which in turn supplies the market participants with valuable information needed for good decisions. This is tied into the accounting system which provides for a measure of value, unlike the socialist accounting which muddies the information flow reaching the market participants. As regards taxation, he states that high marginal taxes tend not to produce higher government income.

The Failure of Socialism and Communism

Russia. As the United Kingdom was successfully undergoing its privatization process, Mikhail Gorbachev rose to leadership in 1985 and called for *perestroika* (restructuring), *uskoreniye* (acceleration of growth), and *glasnost* (openness). Being a leader of the Socialist/Communist world, an example used by many developing nations for patterning their own economic development, this revolutionary change in attitude by the Soviet Union had a tremendous impact on thinking in the developing world. As the Soviet Union began to disintegrate, its influence on the economic philosophies of emerging markets began to dwindle. Russian officials began to talk about liberalization and privatization in addition to cutting government spending in the name of economic stabilization. The Deputy Prime Minister was quoted as saying that the government's budget deficit had to be reduced and the mass of money accumulated over the years in savings had to be organized in such a way that it would be spent in a productive way. The combined impact of the United Kingdom's privatization under the leadership of Margaret Thatcher, and the demise of Soviet communism, had an incalculable impact on development in the emerging markets.

Sri Lanka. These views have now begun to influence policy thinking in multilateral institutions, such as the World Bank, and developing nations around the world. The trend is toward market economies, more predictable government policies, lower taxation, and other innovations designed to stimulate private enterprise. In Sri Lanka, for example, with the change in government in 1977, government economic policy was transformed from the Socialist, centrally planned Chinese/Soviet economic model, which had been pursued by the redoubtable Mrs. Sirimabo Bandaranaike, to a market-oriented model. During their various terms in power, Mrs. Bandaranaike's Freedom party was instrumental in nationalizing almost all of the economy, including the major plantations and industries. This, of course, sounded the death knell for the market economy and economic growth in general. The stock exchange fell into a deep slumber until the economic policy transformation in 1977. In 1990, the stock market was opened to foreign investment, and economic leaders began saying that the engine of economic growth was in the private sector. The objective was to diffuse radicalism among the educated, motivate disenchanted youth by creating jobs, and ensure that economic benefits penetrated to the population at large through a market economy.

Changes in Economic Philosophy

These lessons are not lost on countries around the world. The failure of the economic policies of communism is pointing the way toward a change in economic philosophy in the developing nations of the world, away from Centralist, Socialist policies and toward market-oriented thinking. Ironically, it seems that in the West the trend is in the opposite direction. There is a tendency for central governments to grow larger, and a move toward an economic philosophy that deemphasizes the individual and focuses on the need for the state to be responsible for functions more efficiently and effectively met by the private sector.

As a result of the rapid changes taking place, particularly in the world's largest countries (China, Russia, and India), government reorganization and change is the order of the day. The impact of these changes is difficult to forecast, but the trend certainly seems to be in the direction of market economies. For example, Kazakhstan, which is five times larger than France and a third of the area of the United States, was one former Soviet Republic which successfully made the transition to an independent state. In

1992 it was run by an old-guard Communist leader who had successfully evolved into a popular, elected president strongly in favor of economic liberalism. In 1993, Kazakhstan officials said they wanted their country to become a European Community member. They have used Asia's fast-growing economies as their economic model and consulted with leaders of those economies.

Transformation of China

Probably most important and dramatic is the transformation in China, especially considering that it is the world's most populous country. Although the current government purports to be of the Socialist/Communist mold, in fact a philosophical transformation has taken place in economic thinking. This is having an enormous impact on the economic growth in that country, as central control is being replaced by free-market thinking. Since 1965 China has suffered three major political upheavals, all of which have had significant economic impact. During the Cultural Revolution between 1965 and 1969, the country suffered economic upheaval. During the "Gang of Four" tyranny between 1973 and 1977, the economy again suffered a setback. In the austerity drive between 1988 and 1990, ending in the Tiananmen Square incident, there was another significant economic upheaval. However, following each of these political contortions, the subsequent political and economic liberalization has caused increased economic activity and a rise in living standards.

Economic reforms. China has gradually made a number of important economic reforms, which are having a profound impact. Since 1978 the People's Communes have been replaced by a "contract responsibility system" related to household output. Market forces have increasingly determined prices. Village enterprises in rural areas have been encouraged so that a whole group of new entrepreneurial activity has emerged. Since 1984, the reform movement has moved on to the urban areas. Here, more market-oriented systems were allowed, with the establishment of special economic zones and the opening up of coastal cities to foreign investment and open trade. In 1991, reforms were initiated to rationalize the pricing system, reform the housing and social security system, and open up foreign trade even further. As of 1993, China was opening up its inland areas to the outside world. The emphasis was then to rationalize further economic structures, improve technology and agriculture, try to meet the ever increasing demands for infrastructure such as power plants, roads, and railways, and to install better financial systems for enterprises. Most important of all, the leadership in China recognized that the fundamental resolution of the problems facing the country and further economic growth involved accelerating the pace of reform and the opening of the economy.

Financial changes.   In the financial area, China moved away from a central bureaucracy and allowed the establishment of specialized banks, trusts and investment corporations, universal banks, and various other financial organizations, including security firms. In 1981 the central government started issuing Treasury bonds. This was then followed by the issue of bonds and shares by enterprises. Two stock exchanges were then established, one in Shanghai and the other in Shenzhen, and a nationwide bond-trading system, centered in Beijing, was established.

Demise of Communist education.   In early 1993, it was reported that the People's University of China was abandoning courses in Marxism in favor of business studies. Some 14 new business subjects were being made available at the University, which was originally established by the Communist party to train young revolutionaries. The new subjects, such as real estate management and marketing, were replacing the 17 courses related to Communist dogma that had died as a result of the lack of students' interest. It was also announced that China's Communist Party school, the main center for training young level party cadres, was joining in by announcing that for the first time it would begin teaching China's leaders about stock market operations. These changes represented a radical change in thinking regarding economics in the former Communist nation and were just another sign of the demise of Communist thinking and the rise of free market emphases.

India's Reforms

Probably one of the most striking examples of the change in attitudes toward economic policies could be seen in India in late 1992 and early 1993. From a reliance on state control and central planning, the Indian government is moving more and more toward a reliance on private enterprise. Early in 1993, it was reported that Prime Minister D. Narasimha Rao invited 400 Indian bureaucrats and ministers to a party on the lawn of his official residence. After his guests had had tea, they were welcomed warmly by the prime minister, who then launched into a lecture on the damage to India caused by the socialism advocated by many of his guests.

Liberalization and Privatization in Russia

Until the 1990s, even the thought of a stock exchange was a cardinal sin in Russia; a crime according to the official ideology of the State. In early 1992, Russian officials were saying that liberalization of prices, a move toward the market economy, and privatization were needed. They were then saying that, without free enterprise, there could be no real competition or high efficiency, and no normally functioning economy in Russia. Previously Russia had a totalitarian state system where no responsible person could be blamed. It was a system that did not allow initiatives, and encouraged people to do nothing.

Some observers have said that the 20th century could be seen as an age of failed experiments in socialism, including its Fascist, Communist, and welfare state variants. As the fixation with socialism lessens, they say, we are beginning to see some of the most backward regions of the world turning into the most dynamic. Probably the most important endorsement of market incentives has come from the World Bank, which did a detailed study of its own investment projects in developing countries and confirmed that ". . . market incentives work."

Multipliers of Economic Liberalism

Growing liberalism in many of the former Communist countries has had unexpected and dramatic effects. In many cases, the state regulatory agencies, if existing, are not able to cope with the proliferation of free enterprise. Private companies, in practice, enjoy quite a different business climate than that facing the big state firms. Since the governments are fragmented and administration weak, private entrepreneurs are able to dodge taxes and regulations. Unencumbered by bureaucracy, they are able to make use of newly opened borders.

In Poland, for example, the uncontrolled capitalist sector has already had a large impact. According to some estimates, in 1993 there were about 1.6 million nonagricultural private businesses, of which about 55,000 were incorporated, as compared to state companies, which numbered about 8,000. It was estimated that a quarter of all manufacturing was in private hands. Publishing of both books and newspapers was almost completely in private hands, as were restaurants and shops. About 60 percent of Poles were working in the private sector, and that sector accounted for nearly half of the gross domestic product.

One of the often overlooked ramifications of the global revolution in economic thinking, the move toward a market economy and a more liberal trading and investment environment, is the multiplier effect of the growth in individual country markets on other markets. Now the engines of development are not only centered in the developed countries such as the United States, Europe, and Japan, but are being found in many of the emerging nations, which are multiplying their resources by investing in other emerging countries. For example, large Korean firms are now investing in Russian projects. As of late 1992, several of South Korea's largest corporations, such as Samsung and Daewoo, were planning projects in Russia's communication and electronic industries. In one project, Samsung was planning to have a joint venture to produce city digital telephone stations in the northwest part of Russia. In another project, that company was planning to produce video recorders using parts bought from Russia under a $3 billion credit from Seoul. Another plan was for the Daewoo Corporation to produce passenger buses in a former defense factory in St. Petersburg.

PRIVATIZATION

More and more economists are saying that the keys to growth are low taxes, controlled government spending, a stable currency, open markets, and unrestricted price movements (since such price movements constitute a vital source of information and communication for the economic system). There is also the realization that one of the most effective ways to reduce government spending, and thereby release financial resources for the private sector, is through privatization. Currently in many nations, state-owned enterprises constitute a tremendous drain on the state's resources and budget.

In recent years, the move toward privatization globally, most particularly in the emerging markets, has been revolutionary. An example of how privatization could be successfully launched and implemented was first demonstrated in the United Kingdom during the late 1970s and early 1980s. When the Conservative government, led by Margaret Thatcher, took office, the British economy was declining, and that decline was accelerating. The Conservatives were convinced that a major cause was the extensive government control over industries. They concluded that state-owned industries would always perform poorly, and this poor performance would badly affect the entire economy. The former Labour government had nationalized the coal industry, the steel industry, gas supplies, electricity generation, railways, docks, and a number of other industries. Practically all the telecommunications industry, aircraft and shipbuilding, much of car manufacturing, oil exploration and production, and even silicon chip manufacturing involved government ownership. The nationalized industries showed poor performance with, in some cases, negative return on capital, low productivity, high cost, high prices, inefficient use of resources, and poor service to customers.

John Moore, the person most responsible for much of the privatization in the United Kingdom during that period, said that state enterprises inevitably performed poorly because the priorities of elected politicians were necessarily different from those of the business managers, and both priorities could rarely be pursued simultaneously. Since nationalized industries need not succeed to survive, they naturally tended to perform poorly. He proposed that self-interest, as viewed by the Socialists, was not some evil quality to be repressed, but was simply the urge for people to improve their lives both for themselves and for their families. He said that this self-interest was the engine to progress since the beginning of time, and to pretend otherwise was to ignore one of the most powerful forces available for improving the quality of life for everyone. The British experience demonstrated beyond doubt, he said, that privatization improves the performance of former nationalized industries, and encourages more efficient use of resources throughout the entire economy. He went on to state that there are two equally important arguments for privatization:

- The transformation in attitudes produced by individual ownership.
- The process, which forces politicians to consider and focus on the state's more important role as regulator, and not as an owner, thus making it a more effective overseer of the public's interests.

The Effects of Privatization in Eastern and Central Europe

The former deputy prime minister of the USSR once said that improving the economic situation in Russia could be best summarized in three words: stabilization, liberalization, and privatization. He said that there was a need to develop alternative uses for the savings accumulated over many years, so that they were not only spent on consumer goods, but invested in such things as real estate developments, stocks, bonds, and new private businesses. He summed up the need for privatization when he said that, in the Communist Soviet system, there were no owners, but there were the State's bureaucrats dealing in such things as finance, land, raw materials, legal issues, and approval or disapproval of businesses. This was in contrast to a market economy where the private sector made the decisions.

In Eastern Europe there has been a dramatic change in thinking regarding privatization, and after initial problems the process continues. In Hungary, as of early 1993, 300 companies had been sold for $166 million, including a refrigerator manufacturer, a car manufacturer, and a computer maker. However, there were still 2,000 companies, including a telephone company, pharmaceutical companies, hotels, a department store retail chain, breweries, and oil and gas companies still waiting to be sold. The government was turning to mass privatization after learning that auctioning companies on a staged basis was too slow. As a result of looming government deficits, the urgency to sell off state enterprises to raise cash was appealing. Taking the lead from the privatization launched by the former Czechoslovakia where vouchers were used, the Hungarians were proposing to offer low-interest, long-term loans to encourage small investors to purchase shares in the state companies.

The countries of Eastern Europe face many problems in privatization, since the change represents a shift in thinking and a revolutionary transformation of thousands of companies. There are serious differences of opinion regarding what the objectives of privatization should be. In some instances it is a key to reducing government debt, whereas in other situations it is seen as a way of luring foreign capital. Even in some other incidents, it is a means of releasing entrepreneurial activity. Resistance is great, particularly among those in the state enterprises whose jobs may be at stake. As one official remarked, "I never knew a turkey that has to ask that Christmas be brought forward." After much debate, each country has come up with its own answers.

It is important to note that privatization and industrial restructuring cannot effectively take place unless prices have been freed from control and subsidy distortions. A whole host of reforms must take place, such as foreign trade liberalization and the establishment of a realistic exchange rate. Also important is the need for a legal framework and an independent judicial system. This system should regard competition as acceptable and to be encouraged. Also needed are competitive banking and financial markets to help mobilize and allocate financial resources on the basis of demand rather than central planning. Privatization involves a change in thinking regarding private ownership and copyrights. This in turn is related to ideas regarding how a democratic civil society with personal rights and responsibilities should be established.

The methods used vary greatly, and the scope for variety is great. In Eastern Europe alone there are 27 countries involved, including the former East Germany, the Czech and Slovak Republics, the Yugoslav successor states, and the 15 republics which once formed the Soviet Union. The scale of the work involved is enormous and unprecedented. Privatization is part of a process which is creating a market economy practically from scratch, with all of its legal, commercial, financial, and institutional infrastructure. In the past, for example, most of the total value added into Poland was from the state sector, and for the Soviet Union, East Germany, the Czech and Slovak Republics, it was over 90 percent.

Hungary, for example, is committed to a market approach based on selling businesses for the best price, with no giveaway envisaged except for some price discounts for employees and social security funds. Poland, the Czech and Slovak Republics, Albania, Lithuania, Moldova, Romania, the Russian Federation, Slovenia, and the Ukraine favor a faster process which involves distributing shares widely among citizens either free of charge or for a small fee.

Russia.   As early as 1993, according to reports, Russia's accelerating privatization program was pointing toward having 20 medium and large firms being auctioned off almost every 14 days. By early 1993 the Russian Federation had already privatized 55,000 enterprises and, by the end of that year, its plan called for a total of as many as 50,000 small companies to be sold off, plus 10,000 to 15,000 medium and large concerns. One merchant banker said that, even if the Russian program reached 50 percent of their goal, it would easily qualify as the world's largest privatization program. The Russian privatization program, which began in October 1992, called for one voucher being issued to each of the country's 150 million citizens. The Czech, Slovak, and Polish systems of distribution to the adult public, with investment funds acting as intermediaries, was chosen by Russia as the best route for privatization of large enterprises. The distribution of privatization vouchers free of charge through local savings banks to every man, woman, and child (approximately 150 million people) was begun in late 1992. The vouchers could be used to buy shares directly or they could be pledged to investment funds to buy shares on their behalf. By the end of January 1993, 96 percent of Russians had received vouchers which they could exchange for shares in newly privatized firms at auctions. However, there was no regulatory system to control trading of vouchers and shares and in one case, 350,000 investors were swindled out of their vouchers. Two investment funds, "Amaras" and "Revanche," advertised for people to invest their vouchers in their funds. They promised to pay 120 percent of the voucher face value after one month. But after the promoters collected the vouchers, they fled.

Ukraine. In the ex-Soviet Republic of Ukraine, the second largest ex-Soviet Republic with 52 million people, an ambitious privatization program was launched by 1993. It involved the free issue of vouchers, and the use of investment funds as intermediaries as in the case of Poland and the Czech and Slovak Republics. It is estimated that about 40 percent of the shares in large enterprises would be privatized by that method, with the rest sold by more conventional methods to local and foreign buyers.

Romania. In early 1993 Romania's privatization authorities published a list of the first 162 companies to be privatized as part of its scheme, which was designed to sell off 2,000 small companies over the following two years.

Poland. In Poland, shares in Polish enterprises were being sold to the public as early as 1989, with the companies concerned providing a market in their own shares on a matched bargain basis. In early 1993, the first phase of privatization, involving the selling of medium-sized state enterprises, had been completed with 60 percent of their shares to be allocated to 15 to 20 national investment funds, 10 percent available for free distribution to employees, and the remaining 30 percent to be retained by the state for sale later. This sale would compensate owners of confiscated properties and provide allocations for a proposed national pension fund. In this first phase, the funds would receive an allocation of shares selected on a random basis, and then also be given the opportunity to select companies for further stakes. The second phase of the Polish program consisted of a public distribution of shares in the various funds, with all adults aged 18 and over and permanent residents in Poland eligible to apply for a participation certificate in each investment fund for a nominal fee. The certificates would then be exchangeable for shares in the fund after a transition period.

Czechoslovakia. In the former Czechoslovakia a full program of privatization and distribution of shares in companies was under way in late 1992 and early 1993. The voucher scheme involved distributing books of vouchers or coupons to all Czech citizens over 18 years of age. The voucher books could be purchased for about an average week's wages. The vouchers were worth a nominal thousand investment points, which could be used to bid for shares in the enterprise being privatized, or alternatively could be exchanged for shares in mutual funds or investment privatization funds. In total, 12 million Czechs and Slovaks were eligible to apply for vouchers. While only two to four million were expected to register, in fact more than 8.5 million did so. It is estimated that 70 percent of the people who bought the vouchers handed them to mutual funds. Some of the funds offered to buy back any shares they purchased for up to 10 to 15 times the $35 the customer paid for his or her privatization coupon.

Venezuela. South America has caught the privatization fever and countries from small Uruguay to large Brazil have launched privatization programs. In some cases, the change in attitudes has been dramatic. Carlos Andre Perez was president of Venezuela when the oil industry was nationalized, but by 1993 he was at the forefront of inviting companies back and dismantling the nationalization.

Argentina. Peronist President Carlos Menem of Argentina was known as a nationalist and populist, but nevertheless proceeded with privatization with a passion, despite the fact that such privatization resulted in weakening of union power and layoffs for many workers. Argentina thus made privatization an essential part of its move to reduce government deficits. Even the money-losing, decrepit rail system in Argentina was undergoing privatization in early 1993. Since it was nationalized in 1946 the rail system had been a drain on the Argentinian government's budget. In preparation for the privatization, the government spent about $400 million in severance pay to fire half the system's 91,000 employees.

Mexico. Privatization in Mexico has been very rapid. In the case of government-owned banks, the government transferred ownership of almost the entire banking system in a very short period of time. This was despite the fact that the $7 million market capitalization of the government-controlled banks represented one-third of the entire Mexican stock market. In 1993 the Mexican government was finishing its privatization program by selling 37 more state companies. Up to that time the government had sold or closed 362 state-owned enterprises, with the sales yielding $22 billion. The remaining 37 companies were expected to raise between $4 and $5 billion. In addition to the banks, government-controlled companies in Mexico included television stations, newspapers, cinemas, insurance companies, fertilizer companies, hotels, port concessions, and the airlines.

Chile. The government of Chile started one of Latin America's earliest privatization programs, and between 1973 and the late 1980s sold off some 470 state enterprises, accounting for almost a quarter of the country's output.

Uruguay. In 1993, the government of Uruguay planned to sell the airline and telecommunications company in addition to the electric power generating system. However, when a required national referendum was held, 70 percent of the voters rejected privatization of the government telecommunications company.

Malaysia. In early 1993 in Malaysia, the government announced the further privatization of 260 more government agencies following the successful public offering of several large companies. Dr. Mahathir Mohamad, the prime minister, said that initially government employees resisted privatization, because they thought that it would mean loss of their job security. But now those employees in the government agencies were complaining because they wanted privatization since now they knew it meant increased income plus bonuses and other perks.

Sri Lanka. By early 1993 Sri Lanka, which had been heavily oriented toward government ownership of enterprises, had sold a number of government companies involved in the importation and distribution of motor vehicles, textile manufacturing, the manufacture of ceramics, leather tanning, packaging, hotels, and animal feed manufacturing. Like the program in India, the government in Sri Lanka called their privatization *peoplization* to answer the fear of people who believed that the government might slide back into foreign economic domination, as experienced during the British Colonial period. By 1993, 18 of Sri Lanka's state enterprises had been 51 percent privatized, and another 31 enterprises were at various stages of privatization. In the Sri Lankan program, 10 percent of the shares up for privatization were reserved for the company's employees, 30 percent earmarked for Sri Lankan citizens in the initial offering, and the remaining 60 percent for successful bidders, either foreign or domestic. In some cases, companies that were heavily debt burdened, such as the bus system, were being given away to employees without the state making any money.

From time to time, progress in Sri Lanka was blocked by bureaucrats who said economic liberalization was potentially destabilizing and uncontrollable. However, faced with both Tamil and Singhalese extremists such as the JVP (Janatha Vimukthi Peramuna or People's Front) and the Liberation Tigers of Tamil Eelam (LTTE), the UNP-led government had a sense of urgency. The practical and enlightened former President Ranasinghe Premadasa said, "The engine of economic growth in this decade is the private sector." In order to defuse radicalism among disenchanted but educated youth, he emphasized the need for job creation and penetration of economic benefits to the population at large, and he saw the stock market as a key instrument in achieving that distribution of wealth.

China.   Premier Li Peng of China announced in early 1993 that he wanted to reduce the government's workforce by 25 percent, and to eliminate dozens of government commissions and administrative organizations. In order to avoid laying off staff, the plan was to spin off moneymaking enterprises from the various government organizations and departments. The result was the explosion of business activities by government organizations, often taking advantage of their monopoly position or regulatory powers. In one incident, the government-owned Foreign Enterprise Service Cooperation Organization (FESCO) used their government position to persuade foreign investors to hire local staff through its organization. The company supplied staff and then took monthly fees from staff wages. In 1993, FESCO had 5,800 people working in 1,300 foreign representative offices. FESCO was also diversifying and purchasing office buildings, engaged in a joint venture motorcycle helmet factory with a U.S. company, a joint venture printing plant with a Hong Kong firm, trading companies in Romania and Poland, real estate in Belgium and The Netherlands, a tourist service, a car repair shop, an office equipment supply agency, and other investments.

Turkey. The government privatization program in Turkey, as announced by the Public Participation Administration, was established to minimize state involvement in the economy, accelerate the further establishment of market mechanisms and enhance competition in the economy, decrease financial burdens of economic enterprises, deepen the existing capital market by providing wider share ownership, and provide an efficient allocation of resources. At the end of 1992, 80 companies had been privatized, raising over $1.1 billion, of which $285 million was raised via stock sales in the Istanbul Stock Exchange.

FREE TRADE

It is now widely accepted among economists that more open economies—that is, those that have fewer distortions in their foreign trade regimes—grow faster. Country analyses present overwhelming evidence that open economies grow faster. Now it is realized that liberalization improves existing resource allocation across firms in various sectors, and within firms in a sector. Trade liberalization improves the efficiency of investments by allocating capital to activities that are most profitable. The result is higher GDP growth rates and higher growth rates in productivity.

Lowering of Trade Barriers

The global liberalization of trade has had a profound impact on business and the operation of enterprises. For many years, economic paralysis and stagnant economic growth in many areas owed much to closed rather than open economic practices, such as high-trade barriers throughout the world. Such barriers to trade and technology hindered access to new technology, and perpetuated incompetence and inefficiency due to the lack of exposure to external competition. Free-market policies were revived in the mid-1970s, and the highly protective trade systems which were built up since the 1930s have been slowly dismantled. More and more there is a trend toward policies based on the free entry and exit of capital, reduction of tariffs, and the elimination of quantitative restrictions on imports, the elimination of price and exchange rate controls, and free determination of interest rates. These barriers are also quickly disappearing because strides made in transportation and communications have made such barriers difficult to maintain.

Probably one of the best examples of how free trade has had an impact on economic growth can be seen in east Asia. Countries such as Korea and Taiwan have grown very rapidly as a result of outward looking or export-led growth. This contrasts with the Latin-American countries during that same period in the 1970s and 1980s, which were inward looking and relied on import substitution industrialization rather than on export expansion. Now trade liberalization is spreading throughout the Latin-American region and the majority of Latin-American countries are beginning to overcome their legacy of four decades of import substitution.

Growth of Trade Associations and Pacts

Protective trading blocs were formed in the 1930s following the depression, and were used to protect domestic economies with the expectation that such protection would increase local economic development. However, this growth did not take place, and the economies of those nations which became part of protectionist trading blocs declined. As the trading blocs weakened, they were replaced by the General Agreement on Tariffs and Trade (GATT).

GATT did not stop the formation of regional trading blocs but these new blocs differed considerably from those formed in the 1930s, since they were more outward looking and were not designed to create trade barriers but to facilitate trade. In 1957, the European Community was established, followed by the European Free Trade Area Association in 1960. In Latin America, the Latin America Free Trade Area (LAFTA) was formed, followed by the Andean Pact of Venezuela, Colombia, Ecuador, Peru, and Bolivia, and the Mercosur Trade Pact linking Brazil with Uruguay, Paraguay, and Argentina.

In Asia, the East Asian Economic Group, the ASEAN Free Trade Area, and the Asia Pacific Economic Cooperation Pacts were formed in 1988. In 1989, the Asia Pacific Economic Cooperation or APEC Agreement was reached, bringing together Korea, Japan, the ASEAN nations, Australia, New Zealand, the United States, and Canada. Two years later, in 1991, China, Hong Kong, and Taiwan joined APEC.

In late 1992, the Uruguay Round of trade negotiations, with over 100 countries representing more than 90 percent of the world's commerce, moved toward an agreement targeting a one-third cut in tariff and nontariff barriers. This was estimated to increase global output by some $5 trillion over the next decade. The Uruguay Round was not only concerned with physical trade, but also with rules protecting international property, opportunities for investment, service market opening and generally greater predictability, productivity, and access to global markets.

Growth of Asian Emerging Nations Trading

In the recent past, the emerging nations of Asia have shown consistently the best growth-rate performance. This performance has come largely as a result of their successful export drive to the developed nations. While protecting their domestic economy from too much international competition, they have increased their share of the world's exports and have become efficient and competitive producers. Utilizing large, eager and cheap labor pools and free enterprise-oriented policies, producers in those countries have used their labor cost advantage combined with technology to become major global exporters.

It is also important to note that they have been very effective in harnessing influence within developed country governments, particularly in the United States, to lower import barriers to their exports. One example of their effectiveness was demonstrated when China in mid-1993 launched an aggressive campaign to win "most-favored nation" treatment from the United States by dispatching well-publicized buying missions to major U.S. cities and offering large contracts to major U.S. corporations which could wield influence with the United States Congress and the Clinton administration. This was similar to the successful campaigns Taiwan launched for many years in the United States using the Communist threat to persuade United States political leaders of the need for liberal trade policies toward Taiwan, thus making Taiwan a major exporter to the United States to bolster the anti-communist government.

In Latin America, although their recent past has shown poor growth rates, the gradual abandoning of inward-looking and centralist-oriented policies in favor of more liberal trade, combined with deregulation, has begun to help reverse the slow growth pattern.

MANAGEABLE DEBT

The excesses of the 1960s and 1970s in terms of debt in the emerging markets were beginning to be solved by the beginning of the 1990s. The debt restructuring and bank financial packages started in 1984 were mainly completed by the end of 1992, although there were some countries still under negotiation. The combination of restructuring and improved policies of the debtor countries mobilized support from multilateral organizations and attracted private capital flows, which put the countries in a better position to contribute to debt operations from their own resources. International bank creditors were also more amenable to restructuring, since secondary market discounts on bank claims were falling significantly below the level which the banks had provided for. Therefore the banks were able to book substantial profits by participating in debt-trading operations.

Economic Reforms

Even in Latin America the trend of high government debt and high inflation is gradually being reversed. Economic reforms have created a virtual circle of shrinking government deficits, falling inflation, and a declining debt burden. These changes have been augmented by increased foreign investments, and accompanied by more stable currencies, stronger stock markets, higher exports, and faster growth. The "Brady Plan" debt restructuring, where international banks are prepared to write off some debts in return for the restructuring of outstanding debt into U.S. Treasury collateralized bonds with extended maturities and lower coupons, has had a dramatic impact on the ratio of debt service to export revenues. In Latin America this ratio declined from a peak of 45 percent in 1987 to 35 percent in 1992, thus boosting confidence in Latin America in the world's capital markets. Between 1987 and 1991 there had been a dramatic change in external debt as a percentage of GDP as well (Tables 2–13 and 2–14).

One important way in which the commercial bank debt of the various emerging markets was reduced was through debt conversions relating to privatization. About $40 billion of public sector bank debt was converted to equity claims through official debt conversion schemes between 1984 and 1992.

There has been growing confidence in the emerging markets. Former debtors are now willing to place more money in those markets. The international market for developing country securities has continued to mature with better liquidity, a wider range of currency trading possibilities, longer maturities, narrowing spreads, and an expanding list of derivative products.

TAX REFORM

Will Rogers once said, "Income taxes have made more Americans into liars than golf," and Albert Einstein also stated, "The most difficult thing in the world to understand is taxes." Probably one of the biggest depressants on the rate of capital formation is the risk of tax confiscation by governments. Economists are only slowly

TABLE 2–13
External Debt as a Percentage of GDP

Country	1987	1991
Argentina	73.1	42.1
Brazil	41.4	29.3
Chile	114.8	54.5
Colombia	46.9	38.6
Mexico	76.5	36.4
Venezuela	70.4	60.4

Source: J P Morgan.

TABLE 2–14
Debt Service Payments as a Percentage of Exports

Country	1987	1992 (estimate)
Argentina	73.1	41.6
Brazil	48.1	31.1
Chile	35.5	21.9
Colombia	41.3	31.0
Mexico	42.3	31.3
Venezuela	41.6	21.6
Latin America	45.8	35.3

Source: Institute of International Finance.

beginning to understand that the speed of economic growth is greatly influenced by the amount of income taxes and that there is an inverse relationship between the amount of a country's total tax income coming from income taxes, and its economic growth rate. This is related to the inverse correlation between income tax revenues as a percentage of total taxes and industrial production.

While in the developed world taxation has tended to increase, in the emerging nations there have been significant tax reforms in the direction of lower taxes. In such countries as the United States the tax system punishes savers and rewards borrowers by maintaining large capital gains taxes. By not allowing adjustments for inflation, thus forcing taxpayers to pay taxes on illusory gains, the capital gains tax is transformed into a tax on capital, further discouraging long-term investments.

However, in many of the emerging nations this is not the case, with many countries not collecting capital gains on equity investments and thus encouraging investment and stock market growth. Such policies tend to encourage capital formation and transfer of money from traditional savings to equity investments. In addition, many emerging nations encourage owners of businesses to issue common stock through the stock market by giving tax benefits to listed companies. A number of emerging nations are beginning to realize that by not having capital gains tax they assist growth and development. They realize that capital formation, if not taxed, will grow more rapidly and thus provide more employment. In addition, tax collection in emerging nations tends to be inefficient, thereby inadvertently lowering the percentage of gross domestic product directed to taxes and leaving more money in the private sector for investment.

ECONOMIC GROWTH

Current estimates indicate that the low- and middle-income countries of the world, or the emerging markets, will grow at about double the rate of the developed world. That is, if we take the average real gross domestic product (GDP) growth of all the countries of Africa, Latin America, Asia (excluding Japan), and some countries of Southern Europe (Portugal, Greece, Turkey), the average growth rate is about 4 percent as compared to 2 percent for the developed world. Between 1990 and 1992 the average for the 24 emerging market countries was over 4 percent, whereas the growth rate for the developed markets was 2 percent or below (Table 2–15).

The low base from which these nations are emerging allows for spectacular growth surges. However, the virtuous technology-driven circle, starting from better nutrition and better health care leading to longer life expectancies, coupled with improved education stimulating greater productivity, is now recognized to be the primary structure of relationships behind higher growth. In Eastern Europe the impact of privatization and market liberation is

TABLE 2–15
Real GDP Percentage Growth

	1990	1991	1992
Emerging Countries			
China	+4.3	+7.8	+12.8
Chile	+2.1	+6.0	+10.0
Malaysia	+9.7	+8.7	+8.5
Thailand	+10.0	+8.2	+7.5
Venezuela	+6.9	+10.4	+7.3
Argentina	+0.4	+8.5	+7.0
Pakistan	+4.7	+5.6	+6.4
Taiwan	+5.0	+7.2	+6.1
Singapore	+8.3	+6.8	+5.8
Indonesia	+7.4	+6.6	+5.5
Sri Lanka	+6.2	+4.8	+4.9
Hong Kong	+3.2	+4.2	+5.0
Turkey	+9.7	+0.3	+5.0
Korea, South	+9.3	+8.4	+4.4
Bangladesh	+6.7	+3.3	+4.0
India	+5.6	+2.4	+3.5
Colombia	+4.1	+2.3	+3.3
Mexico	+4.4	+3.6	+2.8
Portugal	+4.4	+2.2	+2.3
Philippines	+3.9	−0.1	+2.0
Greece	−0.4	+1.5	+1.5
Jordan	−0.1	+0.5	+0.5
Brazil	−4.0	+0.9	+0.5
Peru	−4.4	+2.6	−2.7
Average	+4.5	+4.7	+4.7
Developed Markets			
United States	+0.8	−1.2	+1.8*
Japan	+5.2	+4.4	+1.6
United Kingdom	+0.6	−2.2	−0.6
Average	+2.2	+0.3	+0.9

* 1992 estimate.
Sources: J P Morgan; S G Warburg; Morgan Stanley; Smith New Court; *World Economic Outlook*, May 1992; International Monetary Fund; and author's estimates.

expected to be revolutionary, not only because entirely new capital markets are being developed, but because these changes are expected to have a dramatic impact on economic growth.

The reform of capital markets has gradually eliminated one of the great disadvantages of the emerging market companies—the

TABLE 2–16
China: Real GDP Growth

Year	% Change
1985	+13.4
1986	+9.7
1987	+11.0
1988	+10.7
1989	+4.2
1990	+4.3
1991	+7.8
1992	+12.8

Source: *World Economic Outlook*, May 1993, International Monetary Fund.

high cost of capital. As a result of local stock market booms and reform of inefficient domestic financial markets, the cost of capital has decreased, not only because of lowering interest rates, but also because of the ability to raise new equity on rising stock markets. This has enabled these companies to invest more in new machinery and even to begin previously unaffordable research and development activities.

CHINA: THE PROTOTYPE

China represents probably the most typical and most important of the emerging markets today. This is not only because it is the largest country in the world, but also because it is undergoing a fundamental change from being a closed centralized Communist society to an open-market economy. The characteristics that we see in China and the problems facing China are repeated in many emerging market countries around the world.

It is important to note that China is growing at a very rapid pace not only because of recent liberalization but also because of a combination of factors all converging to produce rapid growth. Someone said that it is like putting a dozen Atlas rockets on an ocean liner. Between 1975 and 1984, average annual GDP growth was 7.2 percent with growth accelerating to double-digit levels by 1984. By 1985 real GDP growth had reached 13.4 percent and continued at high levels until 1989 and 1990, when there was a dramatic fall, only to accelerate again reaching 12.8 percent by 1992, as shown in Table 2–16.

China has many of the characteristics of other emerging markets including:

- Expanding educational levels among the population.
- A high savings rate.
- Low wage rates.
- High exports.
- A young population.
- A relatively primitive infrastructure and technology.

This combination of factors is providing the ingredients for higher economic growth rates. For example, the worldwide search for low-cost manufacturing benefits the emerging markets, since the low-cost producers are able to gain a larger market share while high-cost producers are forced out of business. Those countries that have the export advantages therefore build up higher foreign exchange reserves.

Demands Not Fulfilled

In China, as in other parts of the world, particularly in the former Socialist or Communist societies, there is a great deal of pent-up and expanding demand as a result of a "demonstration effect" generated by the availability of more information through the mass media, particularly television, about products in other parts of the world. This demand has not been fulfilled by the low-quality production offered by the state-owned companies. This, combined with significant pent-up savings, results in a potent brew. Some-one has said that the Socialist economies are like a match thrown on a drought-plagued forest, where there has been a long period of economic depression or repression, and a great burst of economic progress is coming just as it has happened in other parts of the world and at other times. The potential demand for goods and services is difficult to calculate but it is clear that once the emerging markets economies are liberalized, there will be an explosive demand for a wide range of goods.

In China as in other emerging markets the workforce tends to be among the youngest in the world; their peak earning years are still ahead of them. In the case of Japan and Europe, for example, the aging workforce means that productivity increases are limited.

Developing the Latest Technologies

As with other emerging markets, China can now adopt the newest technologies and therefore leapfrog many of the existing levels of technology still being used in the developed countries. One of the reasons given for the startling success of the Germans and Japanese after World War II was the fact that they had to rebuild all their plants destroyed during the war and thus could start with the latest technology, while the British and United States were more or less tied to old and less productive plants and equipment. For example, in China and other emerging markets, cellular and optic-fibre technologies now allow for a telecommunication system to be installed in six to nine months instead of the 10 to 15 years required for land-line systems and at significantly less cost.

China, like other emerging markets, has a government that is finding it more difficult to censor and inhibit the free flow of information. Political changes will thus become more transparent and it will be difficult for bureaucrats and officials to control the transfer of information and technology.

Increased Population as a Detriment

Another factor characterizing China and other emerging markets is the relatively greater increase in population. Governments around the world are beginning to realize that unless they allow foreign investments, they will not be able to find jobs for all of the unemployed youths. For example, in China, the rural workforce is estimated at 400 million while only 200 million are actually needed. In 1993 it was estimated that 100 million people were looking for work. Another 23 million people were expected to join the workforce every year for the coming decade. The July 1990 census in China surprised officials when the total came to 1.13 billion rather than the expected 1.08 billion. The underestimation was approximately 50 million people or about the population of Korea.

China and other emerging markets are moving toward manufacturing and away from agriculture. As agricultural productivity
increases, the number of workers needed in that sector declines.
Also, as countries become more developed, manufacturing takes a
larger portion of the gross national product. In China, for example,
manufacturing now accounts for 46 percent of total GNP compared
with 24 percent for agriculture, whereas 30 years ago agriculture
represented 57 percent.

Chinese authorities, as with other emerging market leaders, are
now realizing that they cannot continue to support money-losing
state enterprises, which continue to drain the country's budgets.
In 1992 some economists were estimating that almost two-thirds of
China's 102,000 state-owned industrial enterprises were losing
money. Subsidies to state industries in 1990 averaged about $5
billion a month, compared to taxes collected from state factories at
$2.3 billion a month.

China seems to reflect what some observers state as a worldwide
trend toward free markets and capitalism which is, at least in the
near term, irreversible. World history indicates that such secular
trends tend to move from one country to another and "catch fire."
One example of this is the spread of socialism and communism
around the world after the crash of stock markets in the 1930s. It
seems that economic liberalism and market economies are following this trend.

Chapter Three

Opportunities in Emerging Markets

I nvestors in the United States, Europe, and Japan have increasingly moved from their domestic markets to international markets in the search for higher returns and lower risk or lower volatility through diversification. Emerging market investments are now increasingly seen as fitting those requirements.

HIGHER RETURNS

It is clear to any student of investments that stock market performance is strongly related to the economic performance of the economy. The question we must ask is why should we expect higher returns from the emerging markets? There are two main reasons for this assumption:

1. The economies of the emerging nations are growing faster.
2. The stock markets of those nations are also expanding rapidly.

With shortages of almost every commodity, and an unfulfilled demand for new products as the wealth of the emerging nations grows, the opportunities for businesses can be unprecedented. As demand in those economies grows, the requirements for credit and finance expands, thus stimulating capital and equity markets.

As in developed markets, the performance of emerging markets can vary greatly. Over the seven years ending December 31, 1991, some emerging markets yielded startling returns. Turkey showed a rise of 3,124 percent in dollar terms, Chile a rise of 2,831 percent, and Mexico a rise of 1,978 percent. Over the same period, investors

TABLE 3–1

Performance of Emerging and Developed Stock Markets: 1990–1992 (Total Returns in % of US$)

	1990	1991	1992
Emerging Markets			
Venezuela	+603.2	+48.4	−42.4
Sri Lanka	+112.3	+106.7	−33.9
Greece	+97.8	−18.7	−27.0
Chile	+40.2	+99.2	+16.5
Colombia	+38.1	+191.5	+38.9
Mexico	+30.1	+107.3	+19.9
Turkey	+27.1	−26.9	−45.1
India	+18.3	+18.1	+26.2
Pakistan	+11.4	+172.3	−13.6
Hong Kong	+9.2	+49.5	+28.3
Jordan	+4.4	+15.6	+24.0
Indonesia	+0.2	−40.4	+0.2
Malaysia	−5.0	+12.3	+32.3
Singapore	−11.7	+25.0	+6.3
Thailand	−19.5	+36.1	+42.9
Korea	−25.6	−14.4	+2.6
Portugal	−27.9	+2.3	−19.0
Bangladesh	−30.1	−14.7	+23.2
Argentina	−36.3	+396.6	−26.2
Taiwan	−50.5	−0.6	−26.6
Philippines	−50.6	+59.3	+18.4
Brazil	−65.4	+173.0	+2.5
Peru	—	+114.9	+124.2
China (Shanghai)	—	—	−37.0
China (Shenzhen)	—	—	+6.0
Average	+30.4	+65.8	+5.7
Developed Markets			
United Kingdom	+10.3	+16.0	−3.7
United States	−3.1	+31.3	+7.4
Japan	−36.0	+9.1	−21.3
Average	−9.6	+18.8	−5.9

Sources: International Finance Corporation; Morgan Stanley Capital International; Swiss Bank Corporation; Smith New Court; and Wardley James Capel.

in the London equity market saw an increase of only 341 percent. In the three most recent years, 1990, 1991, and 1992, the performance of emerging markets has consistently provided superior returns than the developed markets. In 1990, total average returns for emerging markets were 30.4 percent versus a decline of 9.6 percent in the developed markets. In 1991 and 1992, emerging markets returned 65.8 percent and 5.7 percent, respectively, while the developed markets returned 18.8 percent in 1991 and a loss of 5.9 percent in 1992 (Table 3–1).

Future Prospects Look Bright

These rises reflect the very low valuations on which individual shares can often be purchased and the rapidity with which changes can occur in the developing world. The opening of new markets, liberalization, privatization measures, and the high savings rates of those markets are all positive factors leading to higher returns.

As indicated above, the various emerging markets indexes throughout the world have shown very high returns. However, a comparison of what actual fund investments have achieved and the broad indexes is not valid since foreign investments in many of the emerging markets have only become practical and feasible in recent years. In 1987 when the Templeton Emerging Markets Fund was started, initial investments were possible in only five countries. We were gradually able to expand the list as our custodial bank serviced new markets and the various governments allowed portfolio investments. By 1993, the investment list had expanded to 22 countries. That list continues to expand as custodial banks are asked by more clients to offer emerging market services and as governments around the world open their doors to portfolio investments.

DIVERSIFICATION

Diversification is a widely accepted principle of investing. Most often thought of in terms of diversification among a number of companies or industries, the value of diversifying among shares from different countries can easily be overlooked. But history in both the developed and emerging markets shows that markets do not move in unison; market leadership changes year to year from one market to another.

For portfolio investors, the need for diversification of risk is great, diversification of assets among many countries and many stocks leads to lower volatility (i.e., lower risk) yet can increase the potential for gain. A broader range of influencing economic and political variables impact on investments across many different countries. When, for example, U.S. investors move from only domestic investments to Canada, Europe, or Japan, diversification increases but the diversification intensifies when they move to such emerging markets as Turkey, Portugal, the Philippines, Malaysia, Brazil, and Argentina. The correlation coefficient of the Canadian stock market indexes and the U.S. indexes have been found to be as high as 0.8, out of a total maximum of 1.0, while, for the emerging markets, the correlation coefficient of the aggregated emerging markets against the U.S. markets is as low as 0.4.

The potential for gain is particularly true among emerging markets where the individual markets tend to move quite independently of each other, providing a great advantage to a diversified portfolio over single country investments. An additional benefit is a low correlation to the world's major markets, allowing the inclusion of an emerging market fund to bring diversification benefits to an overall portfolio.

Of course, these are historical figures, and there is no guarantee that as the world gets smaller with better and faster communications, and as global investors begin investing more in the emerging markets, that these investments will not influence those markets and the correlations between the developed and emerging markets will not increase. At least for the time being, the evidence points to wide discrepancies between market performances at given periods of time.

Perhaps just as important is the wide range of variations and characteristics found in emerging markets, which tend to be more varied than the developed markets. For example, as of December 1992, the average price earnings in emerging markets ranged from −4.4 in Brazil to +36.7 in India. This was compared to a range of +19.7 to +38.9 for the developed markets. Price to book values in emerging markets during that same year ranged from between 0.9 for Brazil and 5.1 for India, whereas the range for Japan, the United States, and the United Kingdom was 1.8 to 2.4 (Table 3–2).

TABLE 3–2
Emerging Markets Valuations as of December 31, 1992

Country	Price Earnings	Country	Price Book	Country	Dividend Yield
Emerging Countries					
India	36.7	India	5.1	Bangladesh	13.0
Colombia	31.5	Pakistan	4.6	Greece	11.0
Malaysia	23.9	Malaysia	3.8	Turkey	8.1
Venezuela	20.0	Venezuela	3.6	Portugal	4.7
Jordan	19.7	China (Shenzhen)	3.5	Hong Kong	4.0
Korea	19.2	Thailand	3.1	Chile	3.8
Singapore	18.8	Philippines	3.1	Thailand	2.6
Taiwan, China	17.2	Taiwan, China	2.9	Pakistan	2.6
Pakistan	16.3	Mexico	2.8	Jordan	2.5
Philippines	16.1	Colombia	2.8	Malaysia	2.4
China (Shenzhen)	16.0	Turkey	2.7	China (Shenzhen)	2.2
Thailand	15.8	Sri Lanka	2.5	China (Shanghai)	2.1
Indonesia	15.5	Greece	2.4	Sri Lanka	2.1
Argentina	14.4	Chile	2.2	Indonesia	2.1
China (Shanghai)	14.3	Indonesia	2.2	Argentina	1.9
Chile	14.0	China (Shanghai)	2.0	Colombia	1.9
Mexico	13.7	Jordan	2.0	Korea	1.8
Hong Kong	13.6	Peru	2.0	Taiwan, China	1.8
Sri Lanka	12.5	Argentina	1.8	Singapore	1.7
Peru	11.3	Singapore	1.7	Peru	1.1
Bangladesh	10.6	Hong Kong	1.6	Philippines	1.0
Greece	9.7	Bangladesh	1.5	Mexico	1.0
Turkey	9.4	Portugal	1.5	Venezuela	1.0
Portugal	9.3	Korea	1.2	India	0.7
Brazil	−4.4	Brazil	0.9	Brazil	0.7
Average	15.8	Average	2.5	Average	3.1
Developed Countries					
Japan	38.9	United States	2.4	United Kingdom	4.5
United States	22.7	United Kingdom	2.1	United States	2.9
United Kingdom	19.7	Japan	1.8	Japan	1.0
Average	27.1	Average	2.1	Average	2.8

Sources: International Finance Corporation; MSCI; HG Asia; and Smith New Court.

EMERGING CAPITAL MARKET GROWTH

The emerging markets constitute a small part of the current total global market capitalization. As of 1992, the total capitalization of the world's three major stock markets (the United States, the United Kingdom, and Japan) was about $7,270 billion. By comparison, the emerging markets only constituted a small portion of the global market at $981 billion. It is important to note that emerging markets, however, are growing much faster than the developed markets. Between 1980 and 1992, emerging markets grew by 577 percent whereas that of developed markets grew by about 258 percent.

The emerging markets, to a great extent, are concentrated in Asia, which is not surprising since the larger portion of emerging markets population and land area is located in Asia. However, Latin-American markets and European emerging markets in addition to, further into the future, African markets, will take a more significant share in the coming decades.

The capitalization of individual emerging markets is small. While as of 1992, Japan had a market capitalization of $2,332 billion, and the United States had a market capitalization of $4,023 billion, the largest emerging market, Hong Kong, had a market capitalization of only $172 billion, while Mexico, the second largest, had a market capitalization of $139 billion. The next largest was Korea, with a market capitalization of $107 billion, and Taiwan, with $101 billion. The other emerging markets ranged as low as $0.3 billion for Bangladesh, and $1.4 billion for Sri Lanka.

However, the potential for growth of the emerging equity markets is great. As indicated by Table 3–3, for the developed markets the ratio of market capitalization to gross domestic product (GDP) averaged 81.8 percent in 1990 with Japan's stock market capitalization almost equal to its GDP and representing 99.1 percent of GDP, the United Kingdom at 89 percent of GDP, and the U.S. market at 57.3 percent of GDP. The emerging countries, on the other hand, averaged 33.3 percent of market capitalization to GDP. In some emerging markets such as Hong Kong, Malaysia, Singapore, Taiwan, and Jordan, market capitalization represented over 50 percent of GDP but in all the other

TABLE 3–3
Market Capitalization as a Percentage of GDP (as of December 31, 1990)

	Market capitalization ($ million)	GDP ($ million)	Market capitalization/ GDP (%)
Emerging Countries			
Hong Kong	83,386	59,670	139.8
Malaysia	48,611	42,400	114.6
Singapore	34,308	34,600	99.2
Taiwan, China	100,710	155,793	64.6
Jordan	2,001	3,330	60.1
Chile	13,645	27,790	49.1
Korea	110,594	236,400	46.8
Thailand	23,896	80,170	29.8
Greece	15,228	57,900	26.3
Turkey	19,065	96,500	19.8
Venezuela	8,361	48,270	17.3
Portugal	9,201	56,820	16.2
India	38,567	254,540	15.2
Mexico	32,725	237,750	13.8
Philippines	5,927	43,860	13.5
Sri Lanka	917	7,250	12.6
Pakistan	2,850	35,500	8.0
Indonesia	8,081	107,290	7.5
Brazil	16,354	414,060	3.9
Argentina	3,268	93,260	3.5
Colombia	1,416	41,120	3.4
Peru	848	36,550	2.3
Bangladesh	321	22,880	1.4
China	–	364,900	–
Average			33.4
Developed Countries			
Japan	2,917,679	2,942,890	99.1
United Kingdom	867,599	975,150	89.0
United States	3,089,651	5,392,200	57.3
Average			81.8

Source: World Bank, *World Development Report 1992*; and International Finance Corporation

emerging markets it was well below that figure with countries' market capitalization representing less than 10 percent of GDP. These numbers indicate that the emerging markets have a long way to go before their full capacity for equity market growth is reached.

TABLE 3–4
Number of Listed Companies

	1980	1992	% Change
Emerging Markets			
Indonesia	6	155	+2,483
Portugal	25	191	+664
Bangladesh	22	145	+559
Thailand	77	312	+305
Hong Kong	137	413	+201
Peru	103	287	+179
Taiwan	102	256	+151
Singapore	103	213	+107
Malaysia	182	369	+103
Pakistan	314	628	+100
Korea	352	688	+95
Jordan	71	103	+45
Brazil	426	565	+33
India	2,265	2,781	+23
Greece	116	129	+11
Sri Lanka	171	190	+11
Chile	265	245	−8
Philippines	195	170	−13
Mexico	259	195	−25
Venezuela	98	66	−33
Argentina	278	175	−37
Turkey	314	145	−54
Colombia	193	80	−59
China	n/a	52	n/a
Total	6,074	8,553	
Developed Markets			
Japan	1,402	1,651	+18
United States	6,251	7,041	+13
United Kingdom	2,655	2,330	−12
Total	10,308	11,022	

Sources: International Finance Corporation; Swiss Bank Corporation; *Euromoney*; and author's estimates.

In addition, current indications are that the number of companies listed on emerging stock markets is growing faster than in the developed markets. Between 1980 and 1992 the number of companies listed on emerging markets grew on an average of 41 percent while the number in the three major developed markets grew by only 7 percent. The growth range in the emerging markets was high with nine countries having well over 100 percent growth during that period while seven of the emerging markets reduced the number of listed companies (Table 3–4).

High Economic Growth

Some observers have said that the growth of security markets or capital markets is directly related to the economic growth of the country. They say that the development of equity markets has helped focus attention on the importance of the efficient allocation of capital, which allows access to capital by new entrants in the economic community, and on income distribution. According to these observers, experiences in the 1970s and 1980s indicate that those countries which have had high economic growth have also had successful equity market development. These observers cite examples such as Brazil, where growth rates fell after policies favoring the equity capital markets were reversed, while at the same time such countries as South Korea, which encouraged capital market development experienced high economic growth. Of course, there are other related factors that tend to indicate such a correlation, since the establishment of an efficient equity market requires conditions similar to those required for a fast-growing economy, such as efficient legal structures and growing educational levels.

It is only in recent years that equity and capital market development has been taken seriously by government planners and multilateral institutions. In the 1960s and 1970s, governments often looked at stock markets as merely gambling dens which drained away financial resources from the "real" economy. Gradually, however, meaningful literature on the subject of the role of capital markets in economic development began to appear, and it was gradually concluded that such markets played a vital role as an allocator of capital and a generator of capital for industrial growth.

Emerging stock markets are expanding at the rate of at least twice that of the matured markets as indicated in Table 1–4. This growth is also being mirrored in trading volumes and the number of stocks listed in those markets. Faster economic growth has resulted in higher savings available for stock market investments. Although from time to time emerging markets are influenced by foreign investors, most emerging markets are dominated by domestic, not international investors, and the dynamic of domestic savings is what is making those markets grow rapidly.

A Significant Change in Economic Policy

In addition, there has been a significant shift in emphasis in economic policy from providing debt for industrial growth to equity. Capital markets are taking an increasing share of the growth in savings, which were previously almost exclusively dominated by the banks. Market capitalization as a percentage of GNP is growing in the emerging markets and reflects this trend. As we have said, the privatization movement has also added significantly to the supply of equities in emerging markets. This privatization movement accelerated in the 1980s and is expected to continue for some time.

More and more emerging market government officials are stating the importance of a stock exchange as a means of providing capital for industry and commerce, and providing a market in which investors can deal in securities. There is a growing realization that more has to be done. For example, in December 1992, President Fidel Ramos of the Philippines said:

> . . . with respect to the goal of developing our capital market, we are still short of the objective. The condition of our securities industry mirrors the economy as a whole—not quite developed and still short of what it could be. This is of special concern to our government today because unless we are more dynamic and aggressive in the business of capital formation, we might as well forget our hope of reaching NIC status in 1998. . . . Let me emphasise this: the development of our capital market is the key priority and strategy of my administration. We realize that investments, both domestic and foreign, are key factors for sustained and sustainable economic development. These investments won't come unless investors are fully assured of a fair and efficient market place.

There is realization that active securities markets provide some competition to what is often a moribund banking system in the emerging world. Securities markets compete with banks in the provision of financing to the private sector, and thus spur the banks to improve efficiency and service levels. These markets also provide the banks with a means to secure their debt in better managed match and risk profiles on their balance sheets. In addition, the success of privatization programs depends on the availability of secondary markets to allow investors to liquidate holdings, thus making their initial investments in privatized companies attractive.

The expanding interest in emerging markets also provides an excellent opportunity for the emerging nations to replace debt with equity, and so ease the burden of interest payments. Unfortunately, this has not been recognized in a positive way by most developing nations because of the remaining fears of colonialism and foreign domination. Attitudes, however, are changing, and more governments are recognizing the value of portfolio investments as a means of attracting long-term risk capital. A number of countries, particularly in South America, have had successful debt-equity conversion programs. Chile has been a leader in this field and, as a result, has not only reduced its foreign debt burden, but has also attracted valuable foreign technology and managerial expertise. Some people cite the role of the equity market in Japan in building an important flow of capital for Japanese companies in the 1960s. In fact, the Japan Fund Inc., listed on the New York Stock Exchange, might be considered the first important emerging market country fund.

DOMESTIC PORTFOLIO INVESTMENT GROWTH

In a World Bank report on social security systems in Latin America, it was concluded that most systems in Spanish-speaking Latin America (Bahamas, Barbados, Chile, Costa Rica, Ecuador, Mexico, Jamaica, and Peru) were decapitalized over a number of years. Social security institutes, even though they were autonomous under public charters, were required to invest exclusively in government bonds that paid negative real rates of interest during periods of high inflation rates. As the real value of their portfolios declined, the funds depended more each year on current revenues to finance current expenditures on health care services, disability, and pension payments. By the end of the 1980s, none of the traditional systems held assets capable of supporting certain future obligations for pensions and survivor benefits.

In addition to privatization of government organizations, countries in the emerging markets are privatizing their pension systems because of their poor investment performance. Chile, for example, has established the trend with a system based on personal pension schemes, whereas in Mexico a law was passed in 1991 to create a compulsory pension fund system to be managed by the recently privatized banks. These changes are expected to increase domestic savings by $1 billion per year. Once the pension funds start to invest in the debt and equity of private companies the reforms could have a significant impact on the stock market, since Mexican fund managers are expected to allocate 50 percent of their holdings to equities and the rest to fixed income.

CAPITAL FLIGHT RETURNS

Capital flight is important in a number of countries. In addition to foreign institutional money, which may be harnessed by emerging equity markets, there is considerable capital flight from emerging market countries which may be attracted back to their home countries under favorable conditions. The World Bank has estimated that between 1980 and 1984, capital flight in Argentina was about $16 billion, $40 billion for Mexico, and $27 billion for Venezuela. In some years, capital flight in Argentina and Venezuela was equivalent to half the savings in those countries. The dismantling of foreign exchange controls combined with the growth of capital markets in emerging nations has resulted in the return of that flight capital in many emerging nations.

FOREIGN INVESTMENT GROWTH

It is estimated that one-half of 1 percent of total pension fund assets in the United States, or about $18 billion, has been invested in emerging markets as of 1993, with more than 50 money management firms having emerging markets specialization. Gradually the investment boards of even the most defensive and conservative pensions funds in the United States, the United Kingdom, and Japan have added *emerging markets* to the lexicon of investment categories which, only a few years ago, included only *equities, fixed income, domestic, international, global,* and perhaps *venture capital.*

Equity investments by developed country investors in developing countries during the late 1980s were mainly through country funds and multicountry or regional funds. However, in 1991 and 1992, the trend moved away from country funds and toward equity offerings by emerging market corporations. According to the International Monetary Fund, in the first half of 1992, international equity issues by emerging market companies amounted to $5.9 billion compared to only $949 million in 1990. One reason for this increase was partly because of privatization in various countries, which required an international market in view of the large size of the issues and the shallowness of most emerging domestic markets. But it also reflected the growing global interest in emerging markets.

Change from Domestic Orientation to Global Orientation

The changing expectations of investors today is best exemplified in the recent history of emerging markets investment development. Emerging markets as a specific investment category has been intimately tied to the changing views of fund managers and investors from a domestic orientation to a global orientation. Even now, the great bulk of money invested throughout the world is invested in the investor's home market. Estimates vary considerably, but it would not be unreasonable to say that only 5 percent of the U.S. pension fund money in 1993 was invested outside the United States. The percentage for Japan was probably less. It is only in the last decade that the fund manager's domestic view has gradually been transformed into an international or global view.

The Surge of the Available Money Flow

The flow of money available for equity markets around the world is growing by leaps and bounds. Just looking at the world's pension fund assets, the growth is significant. According to Intersec Research Corporation, in 1992 total pension fund assets in the world were $5,956 billion, of which $3,315 billion was from the United States, $728 billion from Japan, $644 billion from the United Kingdom, and $1,269 billion from other countries such as France, Germany, Italy, and Spain, who were moving toward a funded pension fund environment. The projection for 1997 is a growth in the world's pension assets to $8,445 billion. Of course, these numbers do not include many countries, which have a government pension fund system eventually to be privatized. In the United States, 5 percent of pension fund assets were invested outside the United States, or about $152 billion, for Japan 8 percent or $60 billion, for the United Kingdom 26 percent or $167 billion, and for the whole world 8 percent or $499 billion. By 1997, it was projected that U.S. pension assets invested outside the United States would rise to 10 percent, for Japan to 12 percent, and for the whole world to 13 percent.

According to another estimate, during the next five years, overall funded pension assets will swell by $2 trillion, of which $500 billion will be added to international mandates. For example, in 1991 alone, the United States recorded $17.5 billion of net new cash from tax-exempt institutions allocated to international mandates. This does not include the large amounts of money held by life insurers who are managing small U.S. company (less than 500 workers) pension money. The pension funds of firms with fewer than 1,000 employees are now estimated to be worth $400 billion.

In early 1993, reports of the flow of funds in the US market indicated huge increases in investors' cash being placed into mutual funds. According to the Investment Company Institute, mutual funds sales in March alone reached a record of $11.3 billion. The first quarter of 1993 showed sales of $60.1 billion, exceeding the previous record by almost a third. It was reported at that time that there was an increasing amount of new money going into foreign stock funds. Investments in shares is also increasing. As of mid-1990, when the New York Stock Exchange conducted its 12th ownership survey, about 51 million individuals in the United States owned shares in publicly traded companies or stocks in mutual funds, a 70 percent increase in 10 years. The study showed that there were over 25 million mutual fund holders alone, nearly four times the total of 1952.

Demands for Better Returns and Diversification

Analysts also expect that the demand for better returns and more diversification will result in more international diversification of funds.

One indication of the changes taking place was when, in December 1991, the Canadian parliament enacted a major budget provision allowing increased foreign (non-Canadian) holdings of all asset classes by pension funds. Whereas previously investments were limited to 10 percent of planned assets, they were allowed to rise to 16 percent in 1992, 18 percent in 1993, and 20 percent in 1994. In Europe, there are plans to expand the single market concept to allow cross-border membership management and investment of European pension funds. The draft proposal made by the Economic Community (EC) Commissioner for Financial Services, Sir Leon Brittan, in mid-1990 would allow cross-border investments by removing investment restrictions such as "buy national" requirements and other portfolio composition limits.

Pension Funds

In line with the move toward more international investments by pension funds around the world, greater amounts are being added to emerging market portfolios. Starting in 1990, according to Intersec, U.S. pension fund sponsors were increasing their exposure to emerging markets dramatically, either by participating in an emerging market pooled fund and separate accounts, or by allowing their EAFE (Europe, Australia, and the Far East) managers latitude to invest in emerging markets. In the United States in 1990, pension funds had about $2 billion in emerging markets, in 1991 about $3.5 billion, and in 1992 almost $5 billion. With total assets of institutional investors in the major industrialized countries currently $7 trillion and growing steadily, even a slight percentage increase in institutional investment in emerging markets leads to substantial additional inflows.

As of late 1992, annualized trading volume on Latin-American solvent loans and loans restructured to Brady Bonds had gone from $1 billion in face value, traded in 1984, to about $200 billion. According to *Euromoney*, between $500 million and $1 billion worth of Brady Bonds were traded daily between New York, London, and throughout America.

Globalization of Equity Markets

The globalization of equity markets is also indicated by studies which show an ever-increasing outflow of investment into international equity markets from the home market. According to one estimate, the worldwide investment in foreign shares increased from $300 billion in 1985 to $1,600 billion in 1989. According to a survey by Greenwich Associates, corporate pension fund managers were planning to increase the international equity portion of their assets to 7.5 percent by 1993, from the average 5.6 percent of 1990.

The 1984–85 recession, induced by the oil price shock, helped create the beginnings of what is now described as the globalization of the world's security markets. The gasoline dollars that were generated by all producing countries had to be recycled, and the recycling of these dollars through the major financial centers of New York, London, and Tokyo created a boom in global finance and trade. This boom required the building of a huge infrastructure of people, telecommunication equipment, and systems, which triggered a growth in the financial services industry.

Foreign Portfolio Investing

Many newly discovered or rediscovered markets have been temporarily affected by the rush of foreign investors who pushed prices up to astounding levels in a short period of time. For example, this happened in Greece in 1984, Portugal in 1986, Turkey and Indonesia in 1989, Venezuela in 1990, and Peru in 1992. The significant characteristic of the experience in Indonesia and

Argentina was the introduction of foreign investors into the market. The inflow of foreign investors and funds acted as a catalyst in both cases to stimulate local investors. We have seen the same phenomenon in many other emerging markets, so that it could safely be said that the introduction of foreign funds into emerging markets has had a significant and largely beneficial effect.

It is thus important for governments in emerging markets to recognize the catalytic effect of foreign portfolio investing in the domestic markets. I emphasize *portfolio* investments as opposed to direct investments, since we have found that many governments have extensive facilities and incentives for direct foreign investments, where, for example, a foreign manufacturer wishes to establish a factory in the country. Many governments give them the right to make the investment, remit profit proceeds, and even enjoy some tax and other incentives. The arguments for such direct foreign investment are accepted by many governments, and include such benefits as technology transfer, managerial know-how transfer, employment for local workers, and export expansion.

CREATION OF NEW STOCK MARKETS

Probably the most exciting aspect of emerging market development in the world today is the creation of new equity markets, particularly in those countries transforming themselves from Communist/Socialist economies to capitalistic free-market economies.

In Eastern Europe, for example, the requirements of privatization have generated great interest in capital markets. Even in Romania, a stock exchange and security law has been formulated and, as of late 1992, a stock exchange was planned for opening in early 1993. Romania's privatization program has moved ahead and, as of early 1992, over 200,000 small private businesses were operating with 8,000 joint stock companies having been registered. In the main privatization program, issue of certificates of ownership in five private ownership funds began in June 1992, with trading beginning at widely varying prices. Stock exchanges are now being run or established in Poland, the Czech and Slovak Republics, Moldova, and other former Soviet Republics.

India.   In India, with a population of 860 million and a savings rate of over 20 percent of GDP, the stock market has grown rapidly. This has been aided by the growth of unit trusts and investment trusts. The Unit Trust of India, which previously had a monopoly until 1987 on the unit trusts market in India, had a retail network of 76,000 agents and over 35 offices throughout the country. In 1992, Indian companies raised 166 billion rupees ($5.8 billion) in primary capital market issues, a 245 percent increase over 1991 despite the fall of the market index.

Pakistan.   In the Muslim countries of the world, the religious prohibition against interest creates a particularly fertile ground for the development of stock markets. In Pakistan, for example, in November of 1991, a religious group declared that bank interest and all other interest was prohibited by Islam in all its forms regardless of whether a loan was taken for productive purposes or consumption. Stock markets are therefore encouraged, and recent liberalization moves by the government have resulted in a massive inflow of funds, not only from domestic investors but from overseas Pakistanis. One young Pakistani told me:

> When the new measures were introduced, I sold my house and all other things I had in America and moved back here. One of my friends transferred $5 million in a single transaction. We are all rejoicing that we can return to our home country and do the businesses we were prohibited from doing before these liberalization measures were introduced.

Indonesia.   Prior to liberalization measures taken by the Indonesian government, the market was moribund. I remember visiting the Jakarta Stock Exchange trading hall, and just a few individuals could be seen holding a desultory bargaining session for a half hour each day. Then, after the government liberalized foreign investments in the market, an explosion of activity occurred. The number of listed companies rose from 24 in January of 1989, to 140 in 1991. Capital raised from new issues during that time was $4.2 billion.

China.   Probably the most dramatic changes and developments in stock markets have taken place in China. Stock exchanges were established in Shenzhen, near the capital of the economic zone to the north of Hong Kong, and in Shanghai. In November 1991, when the Shenzhen Stock Exchange was about to distribute application forms for subscription to 11 company flotations then planned for 1992, over 100,000 Chinese investors from all over the country came to Shenzhen and camped outside the offices of financial institutions in an attempt to get applications.

In the summer of 1992, investors lined up in the city of Xiamen to buy application forms for shares. Investors paid speculators about two weeks' wages for the forms without any guarantee of obtaining shares. Lines of people, some as long as half a mile, formed at the 26 stations selling applications to enter a lottery to decide who could buy shares in four local companies, a car manufacturer, a fishery, and two trading companies. Speculators raised the price of application forms, originally costing five yuan, to 150 yuan in one day. Clearly it was a case of too much pent-up savings chasing too few stocks. In early 1993, the Chinese government announced plans to issue its first foreign currency bonds for Chinese citizens, in an effort to soak up some of the estimated $10 billion in hard currency in private hands.

Shanghai's stock market was keeping pace with China's rapid economic growth, as was the market in Shenzhen, near Hong Kong. More and more state enterprises were being turned into joint-stock companies and many of them were to be listed on the two stock exchanges. In 1992, the number of listed stocks in Shanghai grew to 38 from an original 8 while daily turnover rose to $60 million versus $5 million in 1991. Although, as of early 1993, there were only two stock exchanges in China, the official sources were quoted as saying that other areas in China would be given permission to list stocks on the Shanghai and Shenzhen Stock Exchanges. Chinese companies who obtained tax concessions when they had foreign investors were eager to get their shares listed. Chinese firms with foreign investors paid only 15 percent tax on profits compared to 50 percent if they remained wholly owned by the state.

The rapid growth in Chinese stock exchanges has its precursor in the growth of the Taipei Stock Exchange in Taiwan. During the

10-year period between 1977 and 1987, the Taipei Stock Exchange did not move above 1,000, but then in 1987, it began to ascend with a vengeance. During the three-year period from 1988 to 1990 the index rose from 2,000 to 12,000. While in 1987 the market capitalization of the Taiwan market was $4 billion, in 1989 it rose to $232 billion. At the peak of the market, some of the Taiwan stocks were selling at more than 100 times earnings. The number of brokers rose as the market boomed. In 1988, there were only 28 licensed brokers, but grew to 372 brokerage houses. The number of active brokerage accounts rose from 700,000 to 5.3 million in a country with only 20 million people. It was estimated that one out of every three adults in Taiwan was active in the stock market. This was despite the fact that there was a relatively limited number of companies listed, with the number of companies rising from 123 in 1984 to 200 by 1990.

Chapter Four

Investment Instruments

E merging market investments may be made in four major ways:

1. Direct investment in stocks of emerging markets.
2. Indirect investments by purchases of emerging market companies listed in developed markets.
3. Open or closed-end mutual funds, investment trusts, or investment companies.
4. Depository receipts of emerging market companies.

INVESTMENT TRUSTS AND FUNDS

Some of the earliest investment companies were closed-end funds. In 1822 King William I of The Netherlands created what is now recognized as the first investment trust. It was formed in Brussels, Belgium, to make investments in foreign government loans. In the 1880s similar investment trusts were formed in Scotland and England. One of the oldest closed-end funds is the Foreign and Colonial Investment Trust formed in London in 1868 and still in existence today. This and other such trusts were first derived from trusts formed by wealthy families in the 19th century who appointed trustees to look after their assets. The trusts later became companies so that their shares could be traded widely and more investors could participate. The Edinburgh Investment Trust was established in 1889 and was still in existence at the time of this writing. In March 1889 it was reported that many of the holdings were in what then probably were considered developed markets but which now would be regarded as emerging markets. For example, the Trust had many railway bonds of companies in

Argentina, Brazil, Costa Rica, Cuba, Greece, Mexico, Philippines, Spain, and Uruguay. These railway bonds were yielding about the same yield of the bonds of the U.S. railroad companies, 5 percent to 6 percent at that time.

History of Closed-End Funds. The closed-end funds have had a long history in the United States. They played a major role in the speculative era of the late 1920s. Many investors in this form of fund, which was highly leveraged during the "roaring 20s," sustained major losses in the 1929 crash. As a result, the concept of closed-end funds faded into obscurity for many years. After World War II open-end funds were more popular than closed-end funds. It was not until the 1980s that closed-end funds returned to popularity.

However, in 1951 the Israel Development Corporation was listed in the U.S. market. It was the first single country fund underwritten in the United States. In 1978 it was merged into Ampal-American Israel Corporation. Other closed-end funds formed were the Canadian Fund listed in 1952, and the Japan Fund which was listed in 1962 and was the first U.S. closed-end single country fund of substantial size. In 1987 the Japan Fund became an open-end fund. The Mexico Fund was offered in 1981 and was the first of a long list of other country funds listed. The listing of the Korea Fund in 1984 created a great deal of excitement because of the high premiums that were immediately attached to that fund. In 1985 the First Australia Fund was underwritten, and in 1986, a number of country funds investing in Europe appeared, including the Italy Fund, the France Fund, and the Germany Fund. Also in 1986, the Taiwan Fund was offered and in the next year regional funds began to appear such as the Asia Pacific Fund and the Scudder New Asia Fund. The Templeton Emerging Markets Fund went public the following year.

For closed-end funds in general, there was a bull market that took place in the 1980s. Between 1980 and 1989, 175 new closed-end funds were floated, raising a total of approximately $40 billion. Between 1985 and 1990 net assets of closed-end funds grew from $8.1 billion to $60.9 billion. Between 1989 and the first half of 1992, emerging markets closed-end funds raised $7.5 billion (Table 4–1). They still however represent a very small part of the total fund

TABLE 4–1

Issues of Closed-end Funds Targeting Developing Country Emerging Markets ($ million)

	Developing Countries	Total, 1989 to First Half of 1992
Global funds		365
Asia:		3,862
Multicountry		1,089
Country (specific):		2,774
China		128
India		273
Indonesia		511
Korea		765
Malaysia		442
Pakistan		85
Philippines		253
Taiwan		95
Thailand		212
Vietnam		10
Europe		1,362
Multicountry		886
Country (specific):		521
Czechoslovakia		100
Hungary		180
Poland		150
Turkey		91
Western Hemisphere		1,949
Multicountry		886
Country (specific):		1,242
Argentina		296
Brazil		112
Chile		410
Mexico		324
Venezuela		100
Total		7,538

Source: International Monetary Fund

market since they constitute only about 5 percent of the total over $1 trillion invested in open-end funds.

At the very early stages of emerging market development, closed-end country funds were a popular way of establishing emerging markets and "putting them on the map" among investors in America, Europe, and Japan. By establishing a country fund, investors could gain access and exposure to an emerging market without facing all the problems encountered when entering the markets themselves. In addition, since these country funds were closed-end funds and traded on the major stock exchanges, they were liquid and investors could enter and exit the market rather simply. The most recent survey of emerging markets funds lists 460 such funds with some $22 billion in assets. The list includes both publicly traded and privately placed funds, and both open- and closed-end funds. According to the *Wilson Directory of Emerging Markets Funds*, of the more than 395 funds in existence at the end of 1991, there were 31 global funds, 62 regional Asia funds, 18 regional Latin-America funds, 2 regional European funds, and over 200 individual single country funds.

In some instances, the number of country funds for one country has exceeded even the size of the possible investments in that market. For example, in early 1993, there were over 20 China funds offered with assets in excess of $2.2 billion, but at that time the B shares available for foreign investor purchases in the Chinese markets of Shanghai and Shenzhen had a market capitalization of only $1 billion.

Lipper Analytical Services publishes the *Lipper Emerging Markets Funds Service*, which covers those emerging markets funds that are more easily traded by international investors. The quarterly analysis includes 150 closed-end investment funds listed in the London, Singapore, Amsterdam, and U.S. exchanges in addition to some closed-end unlisted funds. At the initial stages of emerging markets development, most fund managers were reluctant to establish open-ended emerging markets funds. They were fearful that in the face of large redemptions, always a concern with open-ended funds, the relative lack of liquidity in the many emerging markets would create problems. More recently, however, a number of global fund managers have started open-ended emerging markets funds as they gain more experience in trading in the emerging markets, and as the emerging markets themselves grow in size and liquidity.

Open-End Funds versus Closed-End Funds

The differences between open- and closed-end funds are numerous. However, the most important difference is the relationship between price and net asset value (NAV). The NAV of a fund is based on the sum total of all the market values of the fund's securities positions in addition to cash and less any liabilities. The resultant net assets are then divided by the number of shares outstanding to arrive at the NAV per share. Open-end funds or unit trusts, on the other hand, are continuously ready to offer shares to incoming investors at the current NAV plus any sales charges and expenses. They also stand ready to redeem investor shares at NAV less any charges or back-end loads. Closed-end funds must be sold in the market. The important element is that prices of open-end funds are directly related to NAV, whereas in the case of closed-end funds the price is created by the market and may differ from the NAV.

Both open- and closed-end funds offer advantages, the most important of which are:

- Diversification.
- Professional fund management.
- Lower costs.
- Convenience in record-keeping.

The greatest advantage of closed-end funds is that they often sell at attractive discounts to their net asset values. In this way investors may purchase a basket of assets at a discount to their market value. A second advantage is that it relieves fund managers of the worry of possible redemptions and additional money flowing in and out of the funds. In open-end funds there is a tendency for flows into the fund to increase at the peak of bull markets and outflows to increase in bear markets. This could make it difficult for the fund manager to perform at his or her best. However, if investors cooperate with the fund manager and invest more money when the markets are down, then, in fact, open-end funds could be more advantageous than closed-end funds.

Another advantage of closed-end funds or investment trusts is that investors may precisely control the price at which they purchase the shares. In open-end funds, the price at which the shares are purchased is not known until after the investor has made the commitment.

As with all types of financial instruments, emerging markets funds are not freely traded around the world. Each country has various restrictions and requirements regarding investors' purchases of certain funds. However, there is a trend toward global trading of funds as regulatory authorities try to cooperate. In Europe, for example, the USITS regulations were agreed by European Community (EC) participants, therefore allowing funds registered in one country to be sold in other countries of the European Community. Not all barriers have been lifted but Europe has taken a giant step in the right direction. It seems that in the not too distant future, funds, unit trusts or shares, and other financial instruments will be freely traded across borders.

Emerging markets closed-end funds have generally tended to trade at discounts to their net asset value but the range of premiums or discounts have been wide. Generally speaking, those funds traded on U.S. exchanges typically have had narrower discounts and higher premiums than funds listed outside the United States. In addition, there are significant differences between emerging markets funds' performance in view of the wide range of individual market behavior. One significant problem is that during a certain period of time, the emerging markets fund share price performance does not correspond with the portfolio performance of the fund. There is an entire group of investors who concentrate their efforts on only purchasing closed-end emerging markets country funds, particularly those that are selling at large discounts to their net asset value.

In purchasing investment trusts or closed-end funds, purchase prices are listed in major publications. They are sold, just like common shares, with the transactions going through stockbrokers where normal commissions are paid. The key to the valuation of investment trusts or closed-end funds is the discount or premium percentage difference between the share price and the net asset value per share. Other factors to be studied are the percentage of total assets held in cash, the geographical spread of the investments, and the historical total return measured in terms of the performance of shareholders' funds per share.

FOREIGN LISTINGS OF EMERGING MARKET SECURITIES

With the growing interest in emerging markets, some emerging market companies are finding their way to developed stock markets. When the Templeton Organization started the Templeton Emerging Markets Fund in 1987, the range of markets available to us was severely limited. We thus sought companies listed in New York and London that had most of their business and earnings from emerging markets. We found that in London most of these companies were listing such firms as Antofagasta, a diversified Chilean company with major holdings in transportation and mining, and Ottoman Bank, a Turkish bank. Purchases of these stocks enabled us to obtain exposure to the economies of Turkey and Chile whose markets were not yet open to us for direct investment.

As the reputation of emerging market companies has expanded, some firms are now bypassing their own country's often small and inefficient markets to list directly on the major developed country markets. For example, in December 1992, a Chinese firm, Brilliance China Automotive, was listed on the New York Stock Exchange bypassing the possibility of listing B shares on the Shanghai or Shenzhen stock markets, or a listing in Hong Kong. That issue was so well received that the share price doubled and rose from the offer price of $16 to $33. At the end of 1992, the result of this resounding success was a rush on the part of mainland companies to list their firms outside their own Chinese markets in such places as Vancouver and Hong Kong.

International Equity Issues

In recent years the number of international equity issues by developing country companies has outpaced other global equity issues. In 1990, 12 percent of all international equity issues were by emerging country companies. In 1991 that percentage had risen to

31 percent and in the first half of 1992 out of a total $12.9 billion of international equity issues, 46 percent or $5.9 billion were by emerging market companies. Between 1990 and the first half of 1992 a total of $11.9 billion of emerging market international equity issues were made, of which the largest portion of $7.1 billion was by Mexican companies. Other significant issuers were companies in Argentina, Indonesia, the Philippines, China, and Taiwan (Table 4–2).

DEPOSITORY RECEIPTS

Depository receipts are receipts for shares of a foreign company deposited in that foreign company but traded on a foreign exchange. For example, American Depository Receipts (ADRs) are traded in the United States. Normally American banks will have a custodial operation in the foreign country where the shares are traded. The shares are kept in the custodian's vault in that foreign country and then depository receipts are issued against those shares. In the United States, Citibank, the Bank of New York, and Morgan Bank are the largest issuers of depository receipts.

Global Depository Receipts (GDRs) are similar instruments but they are traded in international exchanges. They differ from the American Depository Receipts since they provide issuers with a means of tapping global capital markets by simultaneously issuing one security in multiple markets. Global Depository Receipts can be registered, issued, and traded in U.S. public markets and listed on major U.S. and non-U.S. exchanges. If an issuer chooses to raise capital in the U.S. private placement market, GDRs may be privately placed using the Securities and Exchange Commission's Rule 144A, while at the same time being offered publicly in markets outside the United States.

Prior to the establishment of GDRs, companies were required to issue an ADR in the United States and then an International Depository Receipt (IDR) in Europe when accessing both markets. Global Depository Receipt issues benefit from better coordinated global offerings, a broadened shareholder base, and increased liquidity.

TABLE 4-2
International Equity Issues ($ Million)

Emerging Countries	Total, 1990 to First Half of 1992
Africa	384
South Africa	384
Asia	3,029
China	334
India	150
Indonesia	798
Korea	220
Malaysia	104
Pakistan	7
Philippines	236
Taiwan	461
Thailand	460
Singapore	259
Europe	240
Hungary	90
Israel	60
Turkey	90
Western Hemisphere	8,259
Argentina	622
Brazil	150
Chile	171
Mexico	7,100
Venezuela	216
Total	11,912

Source: International Monetary Fund.

The placement of depository receipts in the United States was facilitated by the Securities and Exchange Commission's June 1990 Rule 144A which permitted qualified institutional buyers to trade privately placed securities without waiting the previously stipulated two-year holding period that generally applied to privately placed securities in the United States. This increased the liquidity of privately placed securities for emerging markets depository receipts. Additionally, some ADRs have satisfied the Securities and Exchange Commission accounting and disclosure rules for listing on the U.S. stock exchanges. The result is that several American Depository Receipts have trading volumes that are now larger in their offshore markets than on the local exchanges.

Depository receipts either in the form of ADRs, GDRs, or IDRs are growing as a means of investing in emerging markets. In 1990, the total amount raised in depository receipts by non-U.S. companies was $2.6 billion, in 1991 it rose to $6.8 billion, and in 1992 to $9.1 billion. Of the $9.1 billion raised and the 46 issues, $4.1 billion was raised in Latin America with 19 issuers and $1.6 billion raised in the Asia-Pacific area with 12 issuers.

In 1992 one leading issuer of depository receipts, the Bank of New York, issued 38 sponsored depository receipts for 16 companies from emerging markets: six Hong Kong companies, two Brazilian, one Taiwanese, one Thai, two Mexican, one Indian, one Venezuelan, one Israeli, and one Argentine company.

The advantage of depository receipts is that they enable investors in America and Europe to invest in an emerging market company without leaving their home market. In many instances, the home market brokerage and other costs associated with purchasing and holding shares are lower in the investor's market. By not going into the emerging markets directly, considerable administrative and other complications are avoided. In addition, dividend collection and distribution is completed much more efficiently since the sponsoring bank undertakes to collect all dividends and then distributes them to the depository receipt holders after converting them into U.S. dollars or the holder's currency.

DIRECT INVESTMENT OF STOCKS IN EMERGING MARKETS

The most rewarding but most difficult method of investing in emerging markets is by direct investment of stocks listed on emerging stock markets. Such direct investments, because of unique local conditions or local investor sentiments, can result in spectacular returns in either negative, but more often, a positive direction. As indicated by Table 4–3, an investment of U.S.$1 in Turkey's stock market in January 1989 would have been worth U.S.$7.34 by July 1990, an annualized return of 634 percent. An investment of £1 during that same period would have been worth £7.21 by July 1990, an annualized return of 621 percent. An investment in Greece in March 1989 of U.S.$1 or £1 would have been

TABLE 4–3
Return on US$ and £1 Invested in Emerging Markets between January 1987 and May 1993

Emerging Countries	Date Invested	Date Sold	Value U.S.$	Annualized Return (%)	Value (£)	Annualized Return (%)
Turkey	Jan 89	Jul 90	7.34	634	7.21	621
Greece	Mar 89	Jun 90	5.58	458	5.44	444
Venezuela	Jan 90	Jan 92	11.34	237	10.80	229
Taiwan	Jan 87	Jan 90	10.18	117	9.27	110
Brazil	Dec 90	Apr 92	3.76	94	4.05	101
Philippines	Jan 87	Nov 89	3.31	82	3.23	80
Argentina	Oct 87	May 92	14.74	71	13.90	69
Korea	Jan 87	Mar 89	2.57	60	2.33	53
Colombia	Mar 87	Jul 92	7.49	50	6.24	44
Portugal	Dec 92	May 93	1.49	49	1.43	43
Chile	May 87	Jun 92	7.17	48	6.14	44
Mexico	Dec 87	Mar 93	10.60	48	11.35	50
India	Mar 88	Mar 92	4.18	43	4.47	45
Thailand	Feb 87	Jan 92	5.27	39	4.55	35
Pakistan	Jul 87	Dec 91	2.82	30	2.41	25
Hong Kong	Nov 87	May 93	3.45	23	4.01	26
Indonesia	Oct 91	May 93	1.48	22	1.68	30
Malaysia	Nov 87	May 93	2.69	18	3.13	21
Singapore	Oct 87	May 93	2.51	17	2.73	18
Jordan	May 89	May 93	1.78	16	1.78	15

worth U.S.$5.58 or £5.44 by June the following year, representing annualized returns of 458 percent in U.S. dollars and 444 percent in pound Sterling. An investment in the Venezuelan market in January 1990 of U.S.$1 or £1 two years later would have been worth U.S.$11.34 or £10.80, annualized returns of 237 percent in U.S. dollars or 229 percent in pound Sterling, respectively.

Of course, these returns are calculated using the market indexes and thus average all companies whether they rose or fell in price. However, correct individual stock selections could have revealed

TABLE 4-4
Comparison of U.S.$ Index with £ Index, January 1987–May 1993

Emerging Countries	U.S.$ Index			St. £ Index		
	Low	High	% Change	Low	High	% Change
Turkey	57	420	+637	32	233	+628
Greece	151	843	+458	89	484	+444
Venezuela	68	771	+1,034	40	432	+980
Taiwan	167	1,700	+918	109	1,010	+827
Argentina	115	1,695	+1,374	67	931	+1,289
Brazil	42	158	+276	22	89	+304
Philippines	674	2,232	+231	441	1,424	+223
Mexico	175	1,855	+960	94	1,067	+1,035
Colombia	160	1,198	+649	100	624	+524
Chile	286	2,052	+617	176	1,081	+514
Thailand	128	674	+427	83	378	+355
India	134	560	+318	72	322	+347
Korea	202	520	+157	132	308	+133
Pakistan	113	319	+182	71	171	+141
Hong Kong	1,086	3,742	+245	593	2,377	+301
Malaysia	84	226	+169	46	144	+213
Singapore	681	1,707	+151	397	1,084	+173
Jordan	85	151	+78	54	96	+78
Indonesia	50	74	+48	28	47	+68
Portugal	330	491	+49	218	312	+43

even more spectacular results. For example. Table 4-4 shows index changes of emerging markets between January 1987 and May 1993. Perez Companc, one of Argentina's largest companies, rose in price on the Buenos Aires Stock Exchange at an annualized rate of 340 percent in US dollars terms and 323 percent in Sterling terms. In the one year between December 1990 and December 1991, the Electrobras Company listed on Brazil's stock exchanges rose in value by 2,900 percent in US dollars and 2,992 percent in Sterling.

PERFORMANCE MEASUREMENT

Performance measurement of mutual funds and investment trusts or closed-end funds involves not only looking at the change in value of the fund's shares, but also the total return of the fund in terms of price appreciation and income. In the case of closed-end funds, it is important to examine not only the market price of the fund, but also the change in net asset value over time, since the two numbers do not necessarily coincide in view of the premium or discount at which the funds may sell in the market. Some analysts prefer to compare the performance of funds against an index so as to determine whether a fund manager has underperformed or outperformed a particular "benchmark" index.

There have been a number of stock market indexes developed for various types of funds. In the emerging markets, the World Bank's International Finance Corporation (IFC) started publishing indexes for various markets as early as 1984. The Morgan Stanley Capital International (MSCI) Emerging Markets Free Index was first published in January 1988, and in 1993 Baring Securities started publishing an *Emerging Markets Index*. There are differences between all these indexes in some or all of the following:

- Updating frequency.
- Exchange rates used.
- Definition of emerging markets.
- Which markets are included in the index.
- Which indexes are used in the overall combined index.
- Country index weighting.

In many cases, dividend reinvestment is not included in the index. Adjustments are made for bonuses and rights issues. At the end of 1992, 18 countries were included in the IFC Index, whereas 12 were used in the Baring Index and 13 were used in the MSCI Emerging Markets Free Index. The Baring and MSCI Indexes were formulated with the purpose of reflecting an index, which would be closer to where an actual investor would be able to invest. Thus they excluded a number of countries where there were foreign exchange or other restrictions inhibiting the inflow and outflow of foreign portfolio investor funds. Such countries included Chile, Colombia, India, Jordan, Nigeria, Pakistan, Venezuela, and Zimbabwe in the case of Barings; and in the case of the MSCI Free Index, Colombia, India, Nigeria, Pakistan, Taiwan, Venezuela, and Zimbabwe. Table 4–5 gives an analysis of the three major emerging market indexes.

TABLE 4-5
Emerging Market Indexes

	Baring	IFC	MSCI Emerging Free
Inception date	January 7, 1992	Investible indexes since Dec 1988	January 1, 1988
Frequency of update	Daily	Monthly/weekly	Daily
Published in	Baring Securities Emerging Markets Index Monthly Updates. Reuters, Bloomberg and Bridge	IFC's Monthly and Quarterly Reviews, IFC's on-line database, Datastream, Bloomberg, FT, and Reuters	MSCI Perspective—Monthly stand-alone database updated with files sent via modem
Index denomination	U.S. $	U.S. $	Local & U.S. $; major currencies possible
Exchange rates used	Reuters quotes at 3 PM London Brazil: Commercial rates; Philippines: Weighted average; Thailand: BOT mid-rate	Most: IFS end-of-period rate; Otherwise: *The Wall Street Journal* (WSJ) or *Financial Times* (FT); if multiple: Free market rates	Reuters verified with Extel and Telekurs; Brazil: Commercial rate
Definition of emerging markets	GDP per capital minimum U.S. $400; manufacturing as percentage of GDP rising; open Market	Low- to middle-income country per World Bank's definition	Low- to middle-income country per World Bank's definition considering investment barriers
Country indexes used	Baring's own indexes	IFC's own indexes	MSCI own indexes
Country indexes weightings	Foreign available capital weighted sector balance and liquidity requirements	Stocks with combined market capital of 60% of total market capital per market capital liquidity and industry classification requirements	Stocks with combined market capital. of 60% of total market capital per market capital and industry classification requirements with a top-down approach

	Baring, as of April 30, 1993	IFC, as of March 31, 1993	MSCI Emerging Free, as of April 30, 1993
Countries included and weighting (%)	Argentina 6.0	Argentina 6.0	Argentina 4.4
	Brazil 13.5	Brazil 10.2	Brazil 13.0
	Chile 0.0	Chile 2.1	Chile 7.4
	Colombia 0.0	Colombia 1.4	Colombia 0.0
	Greece 2.4	Greece 2.3	Greece 2.2
	India 0.0	India 2.6	India 0.0
	Indonesia 2.3	Indonesia 2.0	Indonesia 2.3
	Jordan 0.0	Jordan 0.3	Jordan 0.4
	Malaysia 18.6	Malaysia 20.9	Malaysia 23.5
	Mexico 32.4	Mexico 33.4	Mexico 25.9
	Pakistan 0.0	Pakistan 0.6	Pakistan 0.0
	Philippines 3.7	Philippines 2.5	Philippines 2.3
	Portugal 2.3	Portugal 1.8	Portugal 2.3
	South Korea 5.9	South Korea 3.1	South Korea 3.6
	Taiwan 3.3	Taiwan 1.3	Taiwan 0.0
	Thailand 7.5	Thailand 4.6	Thailand 9.9
	Turkey 2.2	Turkey 4.2	Turkey 2.9
	Venezuela 0.0	Venezuela 0.6	Venezuela 0.0
Adjustments for bonus and rights issues	Yes, using the chained paasche method	Yes, using the chained paasche method	Yes, using the chained paasche method
Dividend reinvestment	Not included in the index	Available in the Total Return index series for all indexes	With Gross Dividend within 2 months

By far the best evaluation of mutual funds performance should include annualized rather than cumulative numbers. Total return is defined as what investors realize from owning a fund, or the change in their investment's value over the time period, assuming dividends and capital gains are reinvested in additional shares of the fund. It is important to see those annualized returns over a period of years in order to understand the performance of a fund. It is impossible to multiply a fund's 15 percent annualized return by five and conclude that its cumulative return was 75 percent since such calculations miss the compounding effect. If, for example, a fund earned 15 percent in one year, $100 would become $115. In the second year, if it earned 15 percent the base would be $115, so the result would not be $130 but $132.25. An annualized return of 10 percent, therefore, would have a cumulative return in five years of 61.1 percent, whereas an annualized return of 20 percent would have a cumulative return of 148.8 percent over five years.

DERIVATIVES

In the emerging market securities, the use of derivatives is limited but does exist in some markets. For example, there are share warrants, options, futures, and share index futures contracts in such markets as Brazil, Hong Kong, and Singapore. However, in many cases the depth of trading is limited.

The most widely used derivative instruments in emerging markets are warrants and convertible bonds. Convertible issues have been particularly popular with Korean, Taiwanese, and Indonesian companies in recent years. The convertible bonds have characteristics of both debt securities and equities. A convertible bond allows an investor to buy a long-term option to convert his or her bond into the underlying common stock at a fixed price. The convertible bond pays interest, just like a bond, and such interest is normally greater than the dividend income that would be received when owning the equity outright. The "strike price" or price at which the bond could be converted into equities is usually significantly higher than the price of the stocks at the time the bond is issued. During a decline of the equity markets, convertible bond prices may not decline at the same rate as the equity because of its interest-paying characteristics.

Criteria for the acceptability of convertibles falls into two categories: (1) fundamental characteristics and (2) trading characteristics. Convertible issues have two major return properties: (*a*) yield, and (*b*) capital gains. Investors may purchase convertibles in order to secure one or both of these properties within a given time frame. When evaluating the attractiveness of a convertible, we must measure the relative merits of both returns. In the yield category, our fixed-income people at Templeton have a number of criteria with which to evaluate a bond and these criteria would be applied.

In the case of our equity specialists, we would want to obtain a yield close to the current rate offered by corporate bonds in the domestic market as well as in the international market. However, even before making these comparisons, we would wish to assure ourselves that there is a real yield. In other words, we want to assure ourselves that the interest rates offered are positive after subtracting inflation. A negative real yield would be an important reason for not even considering investment in a convertible unless the equity portion of the issue had some outstanding characteristics.

For equity investors, the capital gains or equity characteristic of the convertible is most important. In order to make this evaluation, we return to the underlying equity issue's fundamentals. In this exercise, we complete the same evaluation process as we would for any equity issue. This involves comparative assessments, which ask the basic question: "Is stock in this company a bargain?"

We must always be mindful of the issuers' main purpose of issuing a convertible: to obtain better financing terms. The issuer tries to obtain financing at lower interest rates than in a straight bond by offering the conversion sweetener. The buyer then obviously must expect the conversion price to be at some premium to the current market price. If the conversion premium brings the equity price to a level far above the current market price and above its all-time high, the convertible, in our view, becomes unattractive. There are occasions, however, in the secondary markets where we have been able to purchase convertibles with conversion prices close to the market price where even the market price is at a low point. Expectations in this regard, therefore, are not totally unrealistic. Too often, convertibles are offered at the top of bull markets when the underlying equity issue is expensive both in terms of its own price history and in terms of the fundamental earnings power of the company. In such circumstances we do, of course, stand aside.

Warrants are options for a stated number of years that permit the holder to acquire shares at a fixed price (the strike or exercised price), which are normally at a higher premium over the share price at the time the warrant is issued. The warrant can be exercised by surrendering it to the company together with the exercise price. Sometimes warrants are combined with bonds. This occurs when the warrants may be detached from the host bonds carrying them. Typically warrants will trade at a fraction of the price of the common stock, but their price moves in the same direction. Therefore, an investor buying warrants can maintain an interest in a particular equity with less investment than if he or she owned the equity itself. Warrants are particularly common in the Hong Kong market although they are gradually finding favor in other emerging markets. There have been a growing number of offshore listed warrants issued, particularly on South American stocks.

Chapter Five

Technical Aspects

STOCK EXCHANGE CHARACTERISTICS

I f we examine the development of stock exchanges around the world, we find that many of them started as very exclusive clubs of wealthy individuals whose rights to act as brokers were handed down from father to son. Some of these historical precedents are still in evidence today. For example, the Rio de Janeiro Stock Exchange dates back to the 18th century when Brazil was a colony of Portugal. In 1945 the Imperial Government decided to place brokerage business under supervision and control. Brokers were thus classified according to their specialities such as gold, coffee, and securities broking. Originally, brokers were appointed by the government and held office for life. The tradition was perpetuated where the broker license was passed on to the brokers' descendants so that brokerage houses grew into closed family enterprises. This situation existed until 1964 when the Brazil Banking Reform Act was passed and the National Monetary Council and the Central Bank of Brazil were created and assigned tasks to review the regulatory environment of the stock exchange and the security broker industry. The stock exchanges were reorganized under the Capital Markets Law where a number of new brokerage firms were allowed, but even then long-standing brokers were given preference for acquisition of seats within the new exchange although they were required to reorganize from the family structure to corporate entities. In 1976, the Brazilian Securities Commission was established, which marked the beginning of a new era for the stock exchanges in Brazil. In early 1993, there were about 330 brokerage houses registered in Brazil and 9 regional stock exchanges in the major cities.

In Brazil as in other countries, despite new regulatory structures, many of the old structures remain. These systems are difficult to transform not only because of long-standing traditions and habit but also because the institutions operating within these systems and structures profit from them, sometimes very handsomely. Rights to operate as a broker, a custodial bank, a company registrar, or other service organization often means having a monopoly or exclusiveness within a cartel, which can guarantee a comfortable lifetime sinecure. Such entities are difficult to change and are often resistant to the introduction of such innovations as computerized trading, central depositories, book-entry registration systems, and more efficient trade settlement procedures.

Nevertheless, the trend toward more efficient and transparent stock exchange operations is an important one, since it is revolutionizing the way trading of stocks is carried out in many parts of the world, as well as the trading of bonds. In Germany, for example, the Frankfurt Stock Exchange has renamed itself the Deutsche Borse, and is computerizing so as to take a greater share of the total trading in all of Germany. The various other exchanges in Germany, such as Berlin and Bremen, are making moves in order to be competitive and overcome the threat from Frankfurt.

Stock exchanges around the world have begun to realize that instead of the cosy, monopolistic facilities run by club committees and a select group of people, the reality now is that most exchanges are operating in international conditions where there is competition between markets. The growth of depository receipts is evidence of this, and in fact, many investors now purchase depository receipts of foreign issues, rather than trading in the home market, since the cost of trading and safekeeping depository receipts is often less than trading of the original securities in the home market.

The Taurus System

Nevertheless, resistance against reform and change runs very deep, particularly in those markets such as London where traditions die hard. The efforts by the London Stock Exchange to introduce a computerized settlement 'Taurus' system resulted in tremendous losses and the eventual abandonment of the project. The objective of this system was to "dematerialize settlements," so that share certificates could be scrapped and share transfers handled by book entry on a computer. However, the concept of having a central computer maintaining all records of all shareholdings was resisted by the registrars and banks, who were paid to maintain share registers for listed companies and who would have been put out of business by such a system. The resulting concessions made to rival interest groups resulted in the Taurus system turning into a highly complex and impracticable project.

Technically, the challenge is not insurmountable, since airlines and major banks have extensive experience of handling such systems. The Taurus efforts to meet all conflicting requirements, and thus agreeing to a distributed database system using the stock exchange as a hub, resulted in major complications. This project became even more complex when it was considered that de-materialization was a first step toward a rolling settlement system (where all transactions would be settled on a set number of days after they took place, rather than the prevailing London fixed-date settlement system). A delivery versus payment (DVP) requirement would imply the integration of cash and transfer and clearing systems.

Japan's Depository Center, JASDEC

As a result of the similar self-interest of different players, Japanese efforts at computerization are facing similar problems to those found in the United Kingdom. As with London, Japan continues to limp along with paper-based systems that basically have not changed for decades. Japan JASDEC, Japan's depository center, was started in 1984 but actually went into operation in 1991, about five years behind schedule. In 1992, only 2.6 percent of all shares issued in Japan were in the JASDEC system, because of the unattractive fee scale and limited settlement and custody services. Currently, JASDEC only resembles a clearing house rather than a modern-day depository. It does not distribute dividends, proxy, or shareholder rights.

Many emerging markets have the advantage of starting out new in this field, and are thus able to install systems that would be resisted in some of the developed markets in the world. Someone once said that the factory of the future will have only two employees, a man and a dog. The man will be there to feed the dog. The dog will be there to keep the man from touching the machines.

This is certainly a future trend and in many respects emerging markets are leading the way.

SETTLEMENT AND TRADING

Some studies on the costs of maintaining and administering investment accounts indicate that administration, management, and brokerage fees are considerable. According to one study in a $3,000 million pension account, about $1.5 million went for general management and administration, $6.5 million for direct management fees or expenses, $1.5 million for brokerage fees, and $10.5 million for stock and bond portfolio execution costs excluding the brokerage fees. When considered as a percentage of the total portfolio, the $20 million is only 0.7 percent of $3,000 million portfolio. This cost could be considered minimal in percentage terms but, as the size of the fund decreases, the percentage taken by various fees and expenses can be much higher because of numerous fixed costs.

For the securities industry, the trading and settlement of securities faces a major efficiency hurdle. The system requires that investors simultaneously exchange securities for cash under a delivery versus payment (DVP) standard. If the DVP standard is not met, then the investor runs the risk of a late or failed delivery, sometimes loss of securities, which had been paid for, and loss of payment for securities, which had already been sold or delivered. Inefficient clearance and settlement systems therefore present great risk of capital losses, lost interest, and the possibility of fraud and malpractice. Emerging markets, along with some of the developed markets, have major problems in the clearing and settlement of securities. Capital flows into the emerging markets have thus been seriously impeded as a result of improper clearing and settlement systems, and have resulted in the perception by investors that such system failures could jeopardize their clients' investments.

The Group of Thirty

Established in 1978, the "Group of Thirty" is a private, independent group of leading bankers and other financial leaders that has paid particular attention to the global clearing and settlement issue. In 1988, the Group of Thirty experts held a symposium in London to discuss the state of clearance and settlement practices in global markets. Concluding that these practices required significant improvement, a steering committee was assembled to propose a set of practices and standards that could be embraced by markets around the world. The steering committee spawned a working committee of experts who, in March 1989, released a set of nine recommendations to remedy such deficiencies as delayed or too extended settlement of securities transactions, lack of information dissemination to key participants in securities transactions, and other problems in global securities transactions. It made the following key recommendations:

1. The standard settlement period should be $T + 1$ (trade date plus one day).
2. Institutional investors and other indirect participants should be included in the trade comparison system.
3. Central depositories for book-entry transfer of securities should be established.
4. Trade netting systems should be established so that debits and credits between participants can be netted, thereby avoiding excessive payment transfers.
5. Simultaneous delivery versus payment in settlement should be ensured.
6. All settlement payments should be on the same-day basis.
7. A rolling settlement system for all markets should be adapted.
8. Securities lending and borrowing should be encouraged to expedite settlement.
9. The ISO standards for securities messages and the ISIN numbering system for securities issues should be adopted.

Any consideration of what may be expected in the future for global custody and clearing must consider the Group of Thirty and these famous 1989 recommendations, which securities markets around the world should perform for acceptable settlement. Are we close to meeting those objectives? In a word: no. We do not know of any country which has met all the Group's recommendations, but they do provide excellent goals.

Computerized Trading

With the advent of computerized trading, innovations in speed and accuracy are possible, and are being realized today in many markets around the world. Perhaps the most exciting developments are taking place in emerging markets, since these markets are able to leapfrog into the newest and most advanced technology without going through the various stages of development that the developed nations have experienced.

In the area of securities trading, I like to summarize the requirements with the acronym FELT. The goal of all trading systems should be the following: (1) Fair, (2) Efficient, (3) Liquid, and (4) Transparent.

- Fair. Both small and large investors should have equal access to shares at comparable prices.
- Efficient. The trading system must be established in such a way that paperwork is kept to a minimum, and operations are conducted in the most direct and simple way with the lowest cost.
- Liquid. A trading system should foster high availability of shares on both the buy and sell sides. This also implies low transaction costs which enable market participants to be active in the market.
- Transparent. The true nature of supply and demand should be apparent to investors so that they are able to judge the parameters within which they must work when completing their trades. This transparency fosters liquidity, fairness, and efficiency.

I am convinced that the only way to meet the FELT requirements is through the introduction of two important innovations: (a) computerized trading with automatic computer matching of trades; and (b) a central registry, central clearing, and central depository. These two requirements are mutually dependent and both must exist in order to ensure the accomplishment of FELT requirements. The very nature of computerized operations where market participants may enter orders directly into the system enables a fair queuing system, the rapid display of information to participants, on-line operations so that investors may monitor execution of trades to ensure fair pricing, and swift trade execution. In experience gathered around the world, the introduction of computerized trading operations has resulted in a quantum leap in improved trading operations. One example of this is the introduction of computerized trading in Taiwan. When I was managing the Taiwan ROC Fund in 1986, for example, the Taiwan market was, at that time, being dramatically transformed with the installation of a completely computerized trading system. The impact was enormous, not only in terms of the adjustments faced by brokers and other market participants, but also in the impact that computerization had on price behavior and turnover.

The logical consequence of a computerized trading system is an interconnected central registration and depository system, which is also computer operated and linked to the trading system. This enables book entry and central ownership allocation. In the face of such systems, a host of potential problems areas such as counterfeit certificates, lost certificates, and lost payments become avoidable. The impact of such changes on market confidence is inestimable.

However, particularly in those markets where the market participants, banks, brokers, investors, custodians, and government regulatory officials have a vested interest in maintaining the status quo, either because the current system provides employment, yields profits, or imparts power, change will be slow indeed. A number of institutional changes are required and if the participants in those institutions resist, then progress can be slow, despite the recommendations of the Group of Thirty.

A Capital Market System

Progress, however, is being made all over the world, as nations discover that in order to have a healthy economic climate, a healthy capital market system is essential. There are considerable differences in the trading systems of many of the new markets. Traditions, which dominate market practice, mean that considerable adjustments are required by the global investor. Ironically, however, the most interesting complication is the change induced by the new technology. In many of the emerging markets we find ourselves dealing in markets that are undergoing transformation from, for example, floor trading to computer-aided or screen-based trading.

In the clearing and settlement area, investors and their global custodians are faced with local practices, which do not conform to the procedures they normally follow and which, in some cases, they find impossible to follow. For example, some emerging markets have adopted a $T + 1$ system, so that payment is required the day after a trade has been executed. If the investment manager is working in a different time zone and his or her global custodian is in still another time zone, making the $T + 1$ system work requires considerable effort indeed.

Defining good delivery has resulted in substantial delays in entering markets. It is not unusual to enter emerging markets where market practice is to deliver securities days after payment has already been made.

Currency transfer and foreign exchange transactions are another area of complication. Fund managers must carefully monitor exchange transactions when placing money in emerging markets and when remitting payment. Not only must they ensure that their banks are obtaining the very best and most competitive exchange rate, but they must ensure that the transactions are timely. If a transfer is even one day late, it could mean considerable losses when devaluations against the major currencies could run as high as 1 percent a day on a regular basis. In 1992, Brazil's high inflation of over 300 percent annually was reflected in equal multiples of devaluations which had to be monitored carefully.

One example of the problems of settlement and trading came when I visited Poland in 1992. When I met one of the bank officials whose bank also served as a broker, and discussed the possibility of purchasing shares in Poland, the following conversation took place:

Author:
   Well, I'd like to start trading. What should I do? How can we get things started?
Bank Official:
   Well, it's easy. Just open an account.

Author:

Fine, but the way we deal is we place an order first. You buy the stock, inform us by telex, and then we transfer the money.

Bank Official:

Oh, no . . . I don't think that would work because I don't know whether we can trust you to pay up after we bought the stock.

Author:

What's your trading system?

Bank Official:

It's trade date plus one.

Author:

And I said: 'Well, that might be a little tough, but we can do it because we're doing it in Turkey. Are you a member of SWIFT, which is the transfer system that the banks have to transfer money by telegraphic transfer?

Bank Official:

Oh, yes . . . our bank is a member of that system. However, there is one problem. Although the bank can obtain instantaneous notification of payment, the department in charge of the SWIFT operations is in the next building, and it takes them three days to notify us of the payment!

In some countries, there is more than one system for settlement and custodial operations. For example in Brazil, the Rio de Janeiro Stock Exchange has a clearing and settlement system performed by the Camara de Liquidacao e Custodia SA, an independent profitmaking corporation managed by an independent staff which undertakes registration, clearing, settlement, and also operates a fully automated book-entry depository system for securities. However, in São Paulo, the largest exchange in Brazil, settlement and registration is carried by the Vovespa Registered Shares Fungible Custody, a service developed by the São Paulo Stock Exchange (Vovespa). That service consists of share transfer services, custody, and settlement. With two systems operating on the same securities, an additional system is required to link the two.

The Chinese market is a good example of much of what is wrong with many of the emerging markets. In early 1993, these problems included:

1. Listing rules and trading procedures, which were different between the Shanghai and Shenzhen exchanges.
2. Special classes of shares for foreigners which were not fungible with local shares, with A shares for locals and B shares for foreign investors, and different prices for those types of shares.
3. Poor investor communication—in China disclosures of corporate events were not timely or complete.
4. Accounting standards not reaching acceptable levels.
5. A lack of knowledge among the regulatory authorities regarding securities regulations and no clear line of authority or transparency in rules.
6. New issue pricing problems with many equity offerings issued at prices that were far below market acceptance or, in some cases, far above market acceptance.
7. Lack of central depository, clearing, and settlement systems for all classes of shares listed on all exchanges, thus obviating the possibility of a national market. (Since early 1993 the Shanghai Exchange has established a central clearing and settlement and depository system but it is not linked to the Shenzhen Stock Exchange.)

Despite the problems, change is taking place at an ever-increasing pace. Many emerging markets are grasping the challenge to create better working environments for equity markets and installing the world's most advanced systems by taking advantage of the new computer power and software available for such operations. For example, in March 1993, the Kuala Lumpur Stock Exchange started to transfer stocks into its new computerized scripless Central Depository System operated by the Malaysian Central Depository Sdn Bhd. The Malaysian Central Depository was 55 percent owned by the Kuala Lumpur Stock Exchange, 25 percent by the Association of Banks in Malaysia, and 20 percent by a private foundation.

CUSTODY

One of the major problems facing investors when entering a new market is the availability of custody facilities. In the case of international or global emerging markets funds, there is normally a global custodian who is responsible for establishing custodial facilities in each of the countries where the fund is investing. This either means utilizing the local branch of the local custodian bank, or appointing a subcustodian capable of undertaking that function. A great deal of work is required to evaluate the safekeeping system, procedures, insurance coverage, and other aspects, to ensure that the client's assets are safely kept. The custodian is required to follow these procedures:

- Execute buy and sell orders.
- Receive and deliver cash.
- Receive or deliver securities.
- Transmit information regarding corporate actions such as rights issues.
- Collect dividend income.
- Vote per the instruction of the asset holder.
- Repatriate funds out of the country as instructed by the fund managers.

In the global fund management business, there is a careful separation of power between the fund manager and the caretaker of the assets, the custodian. Thus the global custodian chooses the local custodian bank, and ensures that all concerns about trading, settlement safety, and efficiency are satisfied. If there are no local banks with the experience or ability to undertake such work, it prevents the portfolio investor from investing.

Investment managers restricted to only their own domestic market have the luxury of simplicity and directed purpose. The procedures are fixed and accepted by everyone concerned, and custody concerns fade into the background. The term *back office* reflects this attitude. The back office is a place where things "just happen." The term implies the existence of a front office where the real decisions are made to be tidied up by the back office. In the emerging markets arena, however, the back office becomes the front office and is a very important element in the entire investment process.

The process starts with market entry. Emerging markets specialists are often the very first foreign equity investors to enter a market. But before the investor enters, the custodian must penetrate first. We often find ourselves, therefore, prodding reluctant custodians to enter markets that contain all kinds of risks and complications. The transformation in thinking by custodial banks has been gradual for a number of very good reasons. When the emerging markets fund manager asks a custodian to establish operations in Brazil, for example, it is a difficult decision to make when you are one of the many banks that has lost millions of dollars in uncollectable Brazilian loans.

Not least of these complications is the need to meet home-country internal requirements in a new emerging market entry. For example, in the United States the Securities and Exchange Commission requires that approved mutual funds meet a number of custodial requirements, among which is a requirement that any fund assets kept abroad be deposited in banks with at least $200 million in capital. Some emerging markets do not have banks which meet that minimum requirement. Incidentally, I feel that such a restriction is misplaced since a bank's capital size is certainly not a good measure of its safety. We have recently found that: "The bigger they are, the harder they fall."

The question of risk allocation and control has not been fully and completely addressed in the emerging markets area. One reason for this is the existence of emerging markets problems relevant to home-country experience. If we approached a stockbroker in Tokyo and asked what were the possibilities of counterfeit securities in Japan, he would probably look at you in disbelief. However, it is a real possibility in many emerging markets, and a problem that must be confronted by custodians and their clients.

In the corporate action arena, the challenges are great indeed. The first difficulty is identifying the existence of those corporate actions, when they are taking place, and what are the ex-dates and pay dates. Information flows about such matters are not ideal in emerging markets, so that the custodian's task moves to a high level of difficulty necessitating an extra degree of care not normally associated with custodial responsibilities.

Commingling of client accounts by custodial banks presents another challenge to emerging market investors. It is clear that in many accounts in emerging country subcustody banks, assets of different investors are commingled so that in the event of mishap such as counterfeit securities, tracing the actual owner of the worthless securities becomes a major problem. Clients should demand separated accounts to ensure the viability of their holdings.

Chapter Six

Risks

M odern portfolio theory gives a very technical definition of risks. It defines risk as the variance (as measured by the correlation coefficient) of a portfolio's historical returns. Therefore even a portfolio that is yielding excellent returns to an investor may have a high-risk profile as a result of the high variance of historical returns. The idea is to invest in countries that have a low correlation coefficient when measuring market movements between each other. By investing in stocks of countries that have low correlation coefficients with each other, portfolio risk is reduced.

To the layman and to the practitioner there are other aspects and definitions of risk which must be considered. These risks can be summarized as including the following:

1. *Political risks.* The risks arising from a political environment that might lead to an unfavorable or inadequate regulatory situation, political instability, expropriation or confiscation of assets, nationalization, or to such events as exchange controls, which make it impossible to remit capital, profits, interest, and dividends out of the country.

2. *Currency risks.* Risks resulting from a change in the value of a country's currency.

3. *Company or investment risks.* Any risks arising from exposure to a particular company, such as the lack of information, incorrect information, a change in the company's management or ownership, which could affect the operation of the business, or a change in the health of a business, depression in a particular industrial sector, or a sudden price panic.

4. *Broker risks.* Risks associated with exposure to a broker who would jeopardize the investment, such as loss of solvency or

lack of efficiency resulting in share purchases in the market at unfair prices.

5. *Settlement risks*. Risks associated with problems in the settlement of transactions, such as long delays by registrars in registering shares, complicated and error-prone money transfers, or problems in effecting delivery versus payment operations.

6. *Safekeeping risks*. Risks resulting from exposure to local safekeeping agents (custodians) who may not be operating properly, and may be unable to secure adequately the securities on behalf of their clients.

7. *Operational risks*. Risks arising from inadequate procedures or audit standards.

POLITICAL RISKS

The range of political risks is broad and covers the entire gamut of political behavior (or misbehavior!). In some cases, governments try to manipulate stock market prices. Politicians often tend to react to investor complaints and when the complaint is about stock market losses, government officials are urged to prop up the market by using such tactics as asking government-controlled banks or mutual funds to purchase stocks on the market. In Taiwan, for example, the government and political parties have been noted for interference in the stock market. In early 1993, Taiwanese legislators said they were planning to cut the stock trading tax in a bid to revitalize the failing Taiwan Stock Exchange.

In some cases, the governments' emerging markets tend to go overboard in their regulatory fervor and begin to interrupt the market system and functioning. For example, some government regulators attempt to fix fair prices for stocks when they are initially being listed rather than allowing the market to determine the best price. In addition, some countries' governments try to manipulate the market by directly boosting prices when the markets fall dramatically. In Korea there have been a number of instances where the government encouraged purchases of stocks in the market by financial organizations as part of their guidance. In some cases the guidance has been quite explicit with investment trusts and other financial entities being required to make daily reports on the amounts of stock purchased.

Regulation of Securities

Probably the most important task facing securities regulators in emerging markets is how to establish legal structures for investor protection, particularly for the protection of the minority investor. This is important as it means building up the confidence of the general public so that the securities market is seen as a safe place for savings, rather than a gambling den. Fundamental to this role of investor protection is the need to require full, accurate, and timely company financial reporting and disclosure, fair and timely issuance of securities such as bonus and rights issues, fair and transparent trading as well as strictly enforced contract law. One consequence of the gradual recognition of the importance of capital markets and stock markets is the growing tendency in emerging countries to establish more powerful and specialized securities regulatory organizations with the primary role of equity market development.

Probably the best example in recent times of securities' regulation development and the problems thereby encountered may be seen in China, where all the possible problems and the crises involved in the development of the securities market have been encountered, and where the government is just beginning to grasp the importance of proper securities regulation and enforcement. Foreign investors in China decry the lack of an adequate legal framework of clear business and economic laws, lax application of existing laws and regulations, and inadequate court administration. Although the China International Economic and Trade Arbitration Commission has become one of the busiest arbitration centers in the world, foreigners who have won their arbitration awards have not been able to enforce them adequately since the central government courts in Beijing often are not able to make provincial courts enforce their orders or ensure that Chinese official organizations obey the court's judgment. In addition, it is not unusual for judges to favor state enterprises or the government in lawsuits.

The lack of transparency in regulatory procedures is common, with the tendency for special personal connections to hold more weight than the written rule. Very often the rules are not clearly stated and thus difficult for foreigners to follow. This is compounded by insufficient coordination between different government agencies and the lack of explicit information on procedures.

China's Need for an Independent Regulatory Agency

One of the major problems facing China in 1982 was the lack of an independent regulatory agency for capital market operations. Initially, China's central bank, the People's Bank of China, was responsible for regulating and developing Chinese capital markets. However, conflicts of interest were evident from the beginning. Since, in addition to its role as a central bank it also acts as a major universal bank with branches all over the country, the People's Bank of China has its own capital market operations which result in significant conflicts of interests. One observer said:

> The People's Bank of China wanted to control and regulate the securities market but also wants to profit from it by trading in it. Firms undertaking listings on the stock exchanges in China were required to receive approval from the People's Bank. However, there were reports that employees of the People's Bank in Shenzhen and Shanghai were demanding allocations of the highly desirable shares and holding up numerous underwritings. The People's Bank also had an interest in listing companies such as Brilliance China Automotive Holdings which was an indirect, 78 percent owned subsidiary of the central bank's Chinese Financial Education Development Foundation and other affiliates. The Shenzhen branch of the bank had a stake in one of three investment funds and the bank had a stake in a new national securities firm.

In addition to the People's Bank of China's role, the Ministry of Finance, the state-owned Assets Bureau, the state Economic Reform Commission, and the Stock Exchange Executive Council were all involved in stock market regulation and operations in some way that made the regulatory situation even more complicated. At that time, specific areas needing reform included:

- Company law, covering rules for corporate governance and shareholder rights.

- Auditing and disclosure of accounting information in accordance with international accounting and auditing standards, thus requiring improvement of the quality of accounts disclosure and the introduction of automated trading and efficient settlement.

In 1992, one U.S. lawyer involved in the securities business said that the stock exchange in China would continue to expand and would be a great source of funds for Chinese enterprise but added: "It's going to be fraught with potential complications unless the fundamental problems—structure of the system, the regulatory network, and disclosure—are dealt with." Another commentator said: "The lack of a company law describing how to create, operate, and dissolve a company, no unified accounting principles, no strong disclosure system, and no detailed requirements for evaluating a company's assets mean that the markets will have a series of crises during their development."

Restrictions on Foreign Investments

Political restrictions on foreign investment is a continuing problem in emerging markets. Xenophobic attitudes toward foreign investors is not uncommon and a number of countries have restrictions on such investments. Many developing nations cling to past fears of colonialism and foreign domination, shunning portfolio investments from abroad. In the majority of such nations, laws exist which discriminate against the foreign investor. This is particularly true of portfolio or passive investments. While a number of nations welcome direct investments where the foreign partner brings in know-how, management, or capital, many nations bar the entry of capital alone. This deprives local entrepreneurs of the opportunity to obtain capital, not available locally, for worthwhile projects. As a result, some countries are reconsidering their restrictions. For example, they are allowing possible portfolio investments, but allaying local fears of foreign domination by separating voting powers from ownership rights.

Often governments do not differentiate between *direct* investments for purposes of control and operation by foreigners and *portfolio* or passive investments. There is often a failure to recognize the fundamental differences between the two types of investing.

Portfolio investors, for example, do not wish to exert management control over the enterprises in which they invest. By their charters, they are often forbidden to become involved in management, and are even forbidden to sit on the boards of directors of their investments. The reasons are obvious: since their holdings are so extensive and varied, becoming involved with the activities of managements and direction of their invested companies would require an army of staff members, untold number of management hours, and would reduce their flexibility to move from one investment to another.

Some markets distinguish between entry for passive investment only, and entry with the intent of participating in local corporate governance or control. In Pakistan, a fund that intends to vote its shares must execute a power of attorney in favor of the sub-custodian.

Restrictions on Portfolio Investments

In many countries, however, severe limits on portfolio investments prevail. In Thailand, the limitations of what percentage of a company foreigners may purchase has led to a disparity between the price of locally and foreign-registered shares, with foreigners often having to pay hefty premiums for foreign-registered shares when demand is high. When the market declines, the foreigners then suffer a double loss, the stock price declines, and the premium disappears. More importantly, the entire market liquidity is affected since the local shares are deprived of foreign purchases and sales, thus reducing liquidity. Under this system, pricing confusion also reigns. In China, the foreign reserved "B" shares were selling at a discount to the local "A" shares in 1992. The local Chinese investors were thus deprived of shares, which they obviously were demanding since they were paying higher prices for the A shares.

Countries, which fear foreign control and ownership may solve this problem very easily by simply creating a single "golden share" in each listed company that will have the power to prevent control of the company being acquired by foreigners. In this way, foreigners are free to purchase all the shares of a company and thus contribute to the overall market liquidity. In Mexico, foreign-owned shares are sequestered in the national trust NAFINSA so that those shares may not be used for voting. As soon as the shares are sold to local investors, their voting rights are then restored.

Probably one of the more restrictive emerging markets in the world is Taiwan. Despite having the largest foreign reserves in the world (over $80 billion at the end of 1992), Taiwan continued severely to restrict foreigners from its stock market by imposing strict guidelines for investing and making government approval a requirement. A reluctant government will often open the market out of necessity. In early 1992, the Taiwan government's Executive Yuan (Taiwan's cabinet) formally approved a Ministry of Finance plan to open foreign futures trading on 60 futures commodities under six categories. But this was late recognition that such futures trading had thrived underground in Taiwan for many years, making the plan a way to bring the trading under the legal purview of government regulators.

Political and Civil Unrest in Emerging Markets

One of the perceived characteristics of emerging markets is the great deal of political and civil unrest in those markets. There is no statistical evidence to indicate that civil unrest in the emerging markets is any greater than what would be found in the developed markets, particularly when we examine the amount of violence in the United States. Terrorists today are capable of bombing the New York World Trade Center as effectively as they are able to bomb and kill the president of Sri Lanka. The impact of such unrest on stock market investments is difficult to calculate. It is therefore necessary to focus on the degree to which such unrest impacts on the ongoing functioning of businesses and the stock exchanges. Under close examination, it is often surprising to find how businesses can function under very severe conditions of civil unrest.

Probably one of the best examples of the impact of civil unrest on investment can be seen in Sri Lanka in the early 1990s. The country's economic prospects seemed to be closely linked to the war against the Separatist Liberation Tigers of Tamil Eelam. The situation was compared to Thailand in the mid-1970s, when some analysts predicted the Kingdom to be the "next domino" to fall to communist forces after Vietnam, Cambodia, and Laos. However, even when political disturbances were at their height in the mid-

and late 1980s in Sri Lanka, it was business as usual in most of the country, with essential services continuing.

Assessment of political risks has consistently been wrong, and conclusions regarding investments based on simple analysis of political risks is hazardous. Western-style democracies are not a requirement for prosperity and economic growth. Singapore is a case in point. In fact, Western-style democracies are generally unique in the developing world. In Asia, for example, functioning free-wheeling democracies are the exception rather than the rule.

The future of Hong Kong has never been consistently considered to be promising, but I have lived there for 20 years, arriving in 1967 when the Red Guards were running rampant in the Colony. There have been worse times during the last 150 years. The great-grandfather of the current chairman of Swire Pacific, who established that company in 1869, wrote in 1874: "Nothing but loss is apparent." The future was bleak during the Korean War in 1951, there being a physical threat to Hong Kong and the American boycott which killed the entrepôt trade. In 1967, when I arrived, there were serious riots, a collapse of confidence in 1973 and again in 1983. However, Hong Kong's stock market has survived and prospered with dramatic price crashes followed by equally dramatic new price highs.

Regulations of Currency and Repatriation of Profits and Capital

The most common problem when considering an emerging market is the problem of currency regulation and repatriation of profits and capital. In such countries as the Philippines, Greece, and Israel, proof must be presented to authorities of when that initial hard currency was remitted into the country, prior to allowing capital and capital gains to be remitted out of the country. In some cases, records must show the complete chain from initial remittance to the ultimate sale of these specific stocks. For long-term investors, keeping track of these records and ensuring that the local custodian keeps track of such records provides substantial chances for error and involves high record-keeping cost. In other markets currency controls involve the creation of specially designated cash accounts with hard currency to fund settlements.

On a more extreme currency control scale, in some countries currency movements must be licensed by a regulatory authority. In other cases, investors must obtain unique identification numbers that are then used for tax accounting and final ownership controls. Venezuela has such a system and the taxpayer's identification number must be used for every trade. In Korea, the pre-licensing system is in effect and the investment identity card is used not only to track funds for tax and currency purposes but also to determine beneficial ownership. In Taiwan, Colombia, and India, investors must apply for prior approval and documents must be submitted from the investor's country of origin authenticated by a local notary public, and then processed at the nearest consulate before being sent to the invested country.

To be viable for the foreign investor, the entire regulatory and legal infrastructure of emerging markets must provide certainty as to property rights and contract, transparency of trading and other procedures, companies' public disclosure of all relevant information, protection against unfair practices by intermediaries and insiders, as well as protection against the financial failure of intermediaries and market institutions, such as clearinghouses and registrars. In each nation such functions are split among a number of different bodies including the stock exchanges, accounting standards boards, and other organizations in addition to the government bodies. The most threatening conditions are when governments or political factions decide to confiscate businesses and nationalize. It is at such times that investors, particularly foreign investors, are at great risk. Fortunately, the trend of events in the world today seems to be in the opposite direction, with more and more businesses being privatized, and with Socialist, Nationalist, and Communist ideologies declining.

CURRENCY RISKS

Generally speaking in the emerging markets, the trend has been toward liberalization of international payments and transfers. This has resulted from a growing recognition by governments that restrictions on foreign exchange are inefficient and a counterproductive way of achieving the objectives of limiting outflows of foreign exchange, protecting certain classes of imports or exports, and even raising tax revenue. In the former centrally planned economies, particularly in Eastern Europe, payment restrictions have been significantly lifted and currency convertibility has been established with bilateral payment arrangements broadly dismantled. In addition, there has been significant liberalization of capital movements in the developing countries. In Latin America, for example, these changes have been significant. Where previously external financial operations and capital flow were subjected to strict controls, now these controls have been liberalized and in some cases eliminated completely, thus hastening the integration of those countries into the international market.

In the area of exchange rate policy, there have also been major changes, particularly in policies regarding fixed exchange rates with periodic devaluations to more flexible exchange rate policies. It has been realized that exchange rate policies have only a limited effect on real exchange rates and that the real exchange rate is primarily determined by fundamental factors affecting the supply and demand for foreign exchange and is thus independent of exchange rate policy.

However, when investing in emerging markets, it is important to understand how countries' governments try to influence exchange rates. In some cases, the government will try to peg its country's currency to a single currency such as the U.S. dollar. According to some estimates, about one-third of developing countries have a single currency peg.[1] In other cases, countries try to use a currency composite of the major trading partners, so as to make the pegged currency more stable than when just a single currency peg is used. In such cases, currency weights might reflect the geographical distribution of trade and capital flows. There are differences as regards the amount of flexibility allowed in a pegged system. In some cases the peg is rigidly enforced, whereas in other cases varying degrees of margins are allowed. As the liberalization movement gathers momentum, the tendency has been to allow more flexibility and even to have a floating rate within certain

---

[1] Stock exchange brokers use the term *peg* when they wish to prevent the stock price from falling or rising by freely buying or selling at a predetermined price.

parameters. In the case of a "managed float" the central bank will set the rate but will enter the market to ensure the currency trades within parameters they have set based on various indicators such as the country's external payments position, central bank reserves, and parallel market developments. In other instances, an "independent float" is used where rates are fully market determined.

Currency Hedging

Probably the greatest fear of investors in the emerging markets is the fear of currency devaluation and the resultant loss possibilities. Stocks and other such passive investments (e.g., real estate) are thus naturally hedged against relative inflation and exchange rate devaluation. Local investors use investment in stock market equities as a means of escaping the effects of inflation and currency devaluation. Will Rogers once said, "Invest in inflation. It's the only thing going up." However, if an investor is investing in fixed-income securities, then the need for currency hedging could be vital as fixed-income instruments do not adjust to currency devaluations since the returns are fixed. In some emerging markets such as Argentina and Brazil, many fixed-income instruments are adjusted for inflationary effects, thereby acquiring the characteristics of equities.

Recently, there has been a wider acceptance in favor of currency hedging with the argument that investors should fully hedge because currency hedges do not impact expected returns, while they substantially reduce the risks of international investment. The argument is that the currency aspect of international investment is a pure gamble and cannot be adequately predicted. More recently, studies have shown that hedging best applies to short horizons only and that although short-term currency hedging reduces risks, over the long term hedging would not reduce risks at all. Some studies have shown that currency hedging has had a spotty record when used in conjunction with equity investments. One study concluded, "Continuous hedging had the beneficial effect of reducing volatility. Unfortunately, return was also reduced." The vagaries and dangers of playing the currency markets is indicated in a great number of instances.

For example, in early 1993 Malaysia's central bank, which was known as a major player in currency dealing and foreign exchange operations, announced that it had suffered an approximately $1 billion contingent liability on forward foreign exchange transactions. Up to that time, the bank had been known to do more than merely stabilize its currency, by speculating on foreign exchange movements. In 1989, for example, the bank was reportedly criticized by some Western monetary officials for speculating on the yen and the U.S. dollar at a time when the Group of Seven industrialized countries were trying to stabilize currency markets.

The existence of any type of foreign exchange controls presents a considerable barrier to market entry by international fund managers. It adds another element of risk to what is already a risky profession. If there is a possibility that foreign exchange controls may result in our not being able to exit a country or, just as importantly, delay our exit, then we have a considerable degree of risk. A delay could result in foreign exchange losses. In the past this happened to us in the Philippines. With foreign exchange controls in place, the Central Bank of the Philippines required considerable documentation before money was allowed to leave the country. This resulted in delays, often as much as six months. During that time, the bank decreed that the money could not earn interest, thus compounding the risk. So we were sitting on deposits not earning interest with a steadily devaluing currency. Happily, the Philippines no longer has these restrictions and as a result, more foreign exchange is entering the country.

COMPANY OR INVESTMENT RISKS

Perhaps the most essential and highly critical area for foreign investors, or any investor for that matter, is the area of company information disclosure. Many government officials in emerging markets around the world decry the "gambling" nature of stock market trading, but it is no wonder that investors' behavior resembles gambling when they have no information on which to base their investment decisions. If government regulatory authorities had only one task, that task would have to be ensuring that listed companies made full and fair disclosure of company information.

Full disclosure means that all information relevant to the business operations is made available to investors, so that they may make an intelligent and informed assessment of the firm's performance and prospects. Fair disclosure means that the information must be revealed to the entire market at the same time and in the same degree, not only to a few "insiders." It also means that auditors should be made responsible for preparing company accounts that are complete and contain enough detail to reflect fully the operations, problems, risks, and performance as they have been experienced by the company.

Unlike more mature economies, where management is often effectively divorced from ownership, Southeast Asian companies in general, and Hong Kong companies in particular, have been founded and are still managed by individuals and/or family organizations. In many cases, these individuals and family organizations still own a substantial equity stake, frequently between 30 percent and 50 percent of the outstanding shares. While some might view this as a negative factor, arguing that this, in effect, makes them *family companies*, the substantial ownership positions held by the managers align their interest more closely to those of public shareholders. Moreover, the chief executive officers of those companies are more accessible and willing to talk about their company's plans and prospects than their counterparts in more mature economies. Perhaps the more relaxed rules governing the use of "inside information" make CEOs more willing to talk to sophisticated investors.

In Thailand in mid-1987, efforts were made by the shareholders of Mah Boonkrong, a drying and silo company, to ask the company's long-time president to authorize a capital increase to help the ailing financial concern. When the shareholders' representatives met at a hotel belonging to the president's business empire, the lawyer acting on his behalf rejected proxies for large blocks of shares and then ordered the turning off of the lights and air-conditioning in the meeting room!

In Hong Kong, the Carrian scandal rocked the 1981 stock market. In 1979, George Tan had taken over a public company and renamed it Carrian Investments. When the company made an HK$900 million bid for the published net asset value of a listed company, it rose into prominence. It then engaged in a widely publicized deal to purchase an office building for HK$1 billion, reselling it for HK$1.8 billion shortly thereafter. In a short period of time, the company was transformed from one with a net asset value of HK$181 million to a conglomerate of HK$5 billion, after a wild buying spree of all kinds of businesses including an insurance company, a shipping fleet, a hotel in California, a fleet of taxis, restaurants, and so on. It was revealed that Tan used a number of dummy companies and associates to deal and purchase properties from himself, thereby ensuring ever-increasing prices and profits. The complex intercompany transactions, cross guarantees, and uncompleted sales was mind-boggling to the authorities attempting to liquidate the company after the entire scheme was unraveled. The scheme was discovered partly as a result of the Hong Kong property market crash in 1982, during the Sino-British negotiations on handing the Colony back to China. Shattered confidence in the company meant that Carrian could not sell assets to raise cash. Thousands of investors in the listed Carrian shares lost their fortunes as the stock price crashed. Later the company was delisted and declared bankrupt. The result was that 60 of Hong Kong's most respected banking institutions were left with debts reaching U.S.$1 billion. It was also later revealed that Bank Bumiputra, a Malaysian bank established to care for native Bumiputra Malaysian interests, had been lending money illicitly through their Hong Kong finance company to the Carrian Group. As of 1993, trials and investigations were continuing. Two men involved in the case died unnatural deaths. In 1993, a former Bank Bumiputra auditor, who was sent to Hong Kong as an assistant general manager of the bank's deposit-taking subsidiary, was found in a Hong Kong New Territories banana grove strangled with a four-foot belt. John Wimbush, a joint senior partner of Deacons, the law firm which handled some of Carrian's deals, was found at the bottom of his swimming pool with a concrete manhole cover tied around his neck.

Emerging stock markets are also prone to risks of family holdings and majority ownership of related enterprises. When one family company gets into trouble, it may affect the listed company and the interests of minority shareholders. In Indonesia, for example, in 1993, Astra International, the country's second largest company and dominant in the country's motor vehicle sector, got into trouble when the Soeryadjaya family, the company's founder and major shareholders, started selling shares to raise funds for their privately owned bankrupt Bank Summa. Until November of 1992, the family had owned 72 percent of the company's shares but with the problems arising from the family's Bank Summa, and its subsequent order of liquidation with outstanding obligations of U.S.$767 million, the Soeryadjaya family began to dispose of Astra shares, thus putting minority shareholders at a great disadvantage.

The Malaysian government launched a commission to study the securities industry and insider trading. However, officials said that it would be difficult to enforce insider trading regulations since many large share transactions were done through nominee companies. One official was quoted as saying: "The government is actually armed with wide powers to take action against insider trading. It is actually a question of implementing these powers to concerted action."

One example of company risk could be seen when, in 1992, shares were offered in the Chinese market. When foreign investors could purchase shares in Shanghai Vacuum, the first offering of Chinese shares to foreign investors in 40 years, investors rushed in and offered four times more than the $72 million that the company planned to raise in a new share issue. Within a few weeks of listing, the Shanghai Vacuum share price rose to 40 percent above issue price. However, just eight months later, when the company announced a rights issue priced at a premium toward market price, foreign investors ignored the offering and the share price fell 50 percent. By early 1993, the listing was described as the worst B issue coming out of China.

BROKER RISKS

Trading Fairness

The concept of trading fairness implies that each market participant will have equal access to shares at a given price. It means that when a seller offers stock at a given price, all buyers will have access to that offer, and when a buyer offers to purchase, all sellers will have access to that offer. This is almost impossible when there are broker conflicts of interest. If a broker is also acting as an underwriter, corporate financier, or fund manager, and also operating a trading account for his or her own benefit, it is extremely difficult, if not impossible, for him or her to resist the temptation to take advantage of buy and sell orders placed by his clients. When the client places a buy order at a given price, and the market price is lower, the broker may first purchase at the lower price for his or her own account and then turn around and sell it to his or her client at the higher price. It is not surprising, for example, that recently one of the large U.S. brokerage houses announced record profits, the bulk of which came from trading on its own account.

Trading Efficiency

Fund managers try to achieve the best possible returns for their clients. Thus costs must be kept to an absolute minimum. Trading commissions and costs must be low, and this can only be achieved through efficient stock market settlement and custodial operations. Fortunately, with the advent of larger and faster computers, the computerization of stock market operations is making great strides in efficiency possible. This could result in much lower trading costs and greater accuracy. Greater trading efficiency results and lower costs lead to increased trading and liquidity. For example, after Taiwan installed a modern trading and settlement system, trading turnover exploded, while important paperwork savings were achieved.

SETTLEMENT RISKS

Foreign investors are quite concerned about settlement requirements and systems, because any problem in this area could result in defaults, delayed payments, and additional costs. It is for this reason that, when a local stock exchange announces that it will institute a $T + 1$ settlement system, foreign investors raise a hue and cry. This is because, in the global investment arena, fund managers are managing assets from places on all continents.

Instructions for transfer of funds or receipt of securities must thus travel around the world and may originate in time zones quite different from the zone in which the trade was conducted. Each country has a different set of holidays. Delays are inevitable. Foreign investors therefore need a fair degree of time for settlement. We have found that a time frame of $T + 3$ is best, since it allows sufficient time for payments and transfers to be effected, while not being too long to encourage speculation. I believe 14 days, for example, is much too long. But in order for a reasonably tight time frame to be achieved, all elements in the trading system must be coordinated efficiently.

Share Denomination

The share denomination problem raises enormous constraints. In 1992, for example, share certificates in Turkey could be in any denomination, at the whim of the issuer. Therefore you have share certificates of say, 20,000,000, and others of 1,000,000. The unfortunate buyer who delivered the 20,000,000 denomination later could find that they were not salable at the current market price (since buyers want a discount on illiquid instruments) and, in addition, he or she was unable to exchange that large denomination for smaller and more marketable certificates.

Shares in Turkey were also not uniform in their voting and dividend rights. For example, at any time one company may have both ordinary and preferred shares which are divided into Class A, Class B, or Class C (that makes six types of shares). Then again, they were divided into Old, New, and New/New Shares, caused by dividends, bonus, and rights issues that are the result of frequent capital increases at the whim of the company.

Use of Advanced Technology and Systems

Emerging equity markets have opportunities to leapfrog into the most advanced techniques and systems, using the latest computer and communications technology. They are able to learn from the mistakes that have been made in the older developed markets. This holds great promise and has already borne fruit. For example, using the latest computer systems, the Taiwan Stock Exchange has been able to put in place perhaps the most advanced computer trading system in the world. By lowering the cost of trading, this dramatically widened the market for equity investments in Taiwan and created a more transparent market. When further market liberalization allows foreigners to make direct equity investments, the systems will be in place to attract and handle large capital inflows.

Because of the primitive nature of trading on the floor of many emerging market stock exchanges, it is often nearly impossible to obtain timely and accurate price and volume data. This has obvious implications for liquidity. The lack of transparency of pricing also leads to a lack of confidence in the market and inhibits active trading. For example, there are many cases where institutional investors have placed orders of as little as $100,000 and it has taken weeks for the market to absorb this amount. Investors require a market that can handle orders in sizes of millions. Such a market requires a modern, computerized trading system such as those found in Taiwan and Singapore.

SAFEKEEPING RISKS

More and more custodians are coming under scrutiny regarding their role as guardians of assets, and also as the record-keepers of stock movements and corporate actions. There is sometimes a debate about which method should be used regarding custodial responsibilities—having an independent custodian, or having the fund manager provide custody services in-house as part of an integrated service. In the latter case, it must be ensured that the two activities are independently regulated, and separately contracted and managed. In the case of fraud, an independent custodian is an extra guarantee that the reasons for problems will be uncovered unless, of course, the custodian is undertaking the fraudulent activities.

Fraud and Coruption in Stock Markets

There have been a number cases of fraud and corruption in stock markets in the emerging markets. In March 1993 in Indonesia, for example, in Bapepam, the regulatory agency in Indonesia, suspended trading on five major stocks because fraudulent shares were discovered in four brokerage houses. The Indonesian government started the search for two individuals, executives of a small trading company, who were suspected of masterminding the fake share scam. Newspaper reports indicated that the extent of the fraud shares was approximately $5 million. The criminals sold shares directly to brokers including a number of foreign brokers. The counterfeit share certificates, according to press reports, were of exceptional quality and passed ultraviolet tests for watermarks and carried authentic names and numbers. They also had a convincing history of past transactions with brokers' stamps recording trades on the reverse side, indicating that brokers' stamps had been forged as well. Later the stock exchange in Jakarta admitted that during a certain period even genuine share certificates did not comply with the security printing standards set up by the government. A market discussion was held regarding what should be done in the future, and it was concluded that the best solution would be a shift to paperless settlement. One market observer said that the stock exchange management was slow to endorse such a move since it might expose the true scale of counterfeit or duplicate shares when everyone was required to register their shares.

Malaysia. In the Malaysian Kuala Lumpur Stock Exchange in 1992, there was a scandal surrounding the *mislaying* of 75,000 certificates representing 75 million shares. The confusion was a result of a rapidly expanding stock market and hectic trading.

Greece. In 1991, a stock exchange in Greece suspended trading in Titan Cement, a leading blue-chip stock, following the discovery of several thousand forged certificates. Two Greek lawyers and a trader were arrested on charges of circulating the forged share certificates. The scandal exposed weaknesses in the stock market legal framework, which did not spell out responsibilities for fraud and forgery.

Turkey. In 1990, the Istanbul Stock Exchange announced the existence of counterfeit share certificates in Curkurova. A number of local and foreign investors held shares and discovered counterfeit shares in their portfolios. Initially the ISE brokers and custodians denied responsibility and it was not until a year after the event that compensation was made by the stock exchange.

India. During 1992, there was a major scandal involving millions of dollars. In early April of that year, officials of the State Bank of India discovered that security records for government securities transactions had been falsified, leaving the bank short of millions of dollars. A number of foreign banks, including international houses such as Citibank and Standard Chartered, were involved in the trading of government-backed bonds, including those issued by state-owned companies. Trading rapidly expanded as price fluctuations and interest rates increased from 1990 to early 1992. However, because of the inefficient and sluggish transfer operations of the actual bonds, banks began to trade receipts for the bonds with promises to deliver the actual bonds later. Trading volumes became huge and some operators began issuing receipts without any supporting assets, using the money to play the booming stock market. The false receipts were traded as genuine receipts and thus there were not enough bonds to redeem all the receipts. When the final dénouement came, the gap was $1.3 billion. According to investigators, much of the illegal money that had sent the stock market to record highs had been lent by banks on the collateral of bank receipts that could not be redeemed.

OPERATIONAL RISKS

In the ideal world, emerging countries should offer investors equity markets, which have:

- An organizational structure, understandable to both the domestic and international investors.
- An efficient, transparent, and low-cost trading system.
- A settlement and custodial system which enables simple and safe operations for the transfer of securities.
- The availability of timely and reliable company information, so that reasoned and informed investment decisions may be made.

The range of requirements relating to entry and exit of assets from one country to another is great in the emerging markets. In most markets, some form of record-keeping is required when currency enters the country and when it exits. In Greece for example, custodial banks must keep records of each conversion of currency to prove that funds being sent out were earlier received from inward movements.

The Control of Currency

At the next level of currency control are markets where investors must create special designated cash accounts with hard currency to settle trades. This is the case in Bangladesh and Sri Lanka, for example. In the most restricted countries, each movement of currency in and out of the country must be licensed by a regulatory authority. This is particularly true in some of the East European countries such as Hungary and Poland. Some markets require that a unique identification number be obtained by the investor which could be used for foreign ownership control and tax accounting. In Korea, for example, an investment identity card must be obtained for tax and currency control purposes as well as for tracking beneficial ownership by foreign investors. There are different varieties of complexities for various countries. For example, in Taiwan, specific permission must be obtained and the investment must enter the country within a certain time period. Then a separate application must be made to exit the country with capital and profits. In many countries, complicated sets of documents must be submitted and each document must be authenticated by local notary publics and consularized by the country's consulate overseas. Some markets require the use of local agents who act to approve payments and prepare reports for the foreign investors. Of course, these services add to the cost.

Entry and exit regulations are changing continuously in the 1990s. Initially, when Brazil and Korea opened to foreign investment, a plethora of regulations and restrictions were instituted and local agents were required in addition to the custodians. Gradually, these regulations and restrictions were relaxed.

In 1992, the Turkish organizational structure for capital markets was confused and without clear lines of responsibility and authority. The Capital Markets Board (CMB) and the Istanbul Stock Exchange (ISE) both seemed to have overlapping authority and responsibilities while, at the same time, they were not covering essential aspects of capital market operations at all. As a result of this, progress on the stock exchange's development suffered. Fast and efficient implementation of such key matters as trading and settlement computerization, formation of a central depository, and extension of trading hours and settlement dates were not resolved to the satisfaction of both domestic and international investors. For five years, there was no resolution and implementation in regard to establishing a central depository or computerization of trading which would make trading more transparent and efficient. Thankfully, these conditions are changing in Turkey.

Another important difference is that investors need to be able to liquidate their holdings at short notice, and often quite frequently. The bulk of international portfolio investments are made on behalf of pension funds and open-ended mutual funds of unit trusts, where shareholder or pensioner redemptions are constantly received, and where the fund manager is committed to honor such requests on demand. The portfolio turnover of some unit trusts, for example, has averaged about 50 percent per year. This means that the average holding period has been two years. But it would not be unusual for a fund manager to buy and sell investments in one country in as short a time period as a week, especially under conditions where redemption requests require such turnover, or the investment criteria demanded it.

Market entry requirements evolve constantly. For example, when Brazil, Korea, and Chile first opened to nonresident investment, they insisted that foreign funds employ local agents who were entirely distinct from the funds' custodians. Now, the agent's role there is carried out essentially pro forma as a part of the normal custody process. This shows that gatekeeping entry requirements, such as those outlined above, tend to fade over time, leaving only effectively open markets in their wake.

The Lack of Liquidity

The lack of liquidity in many of the emerging stock markets is a source of major problems for foreign portfolio investors. If, for example, an investor had about $2 billion in emerging markets money under management, let us assume that there were 200 companies in the portfolio, or an average of $10 million per company. If the manager tried to dispose of one of those companies, how long would it take to do so without disturbing the price, when daily trading of that company amounted to only $100,000—not an unusual occurrence in emerging markets?

In August 1992, more than 1 million people jammed 350,000 distribution centers in Shenzhen, China, to seek a chance to buy shares. Officials of the Shenzhen Stock Exchange and others were involved in massive fraud in the distribution of share application forms. As a result, 9 people, including Communist party members and police officers, were punished; and 21 people were arrested for allegedly scouting forms, reselling fake applications and selling fake exchange certificates. Rioting erupted when some would-be investors accused bank officials and other authorities of hoarding application forms and reselling them for up to five times their face value. It is estimated that a total of 105,000 forms were sold privately.

Undeveloped Rules and Regulations

In many of the emerging markets, regulation and surveillance of trading systems as well as the general regulatory framework have not been fully developed. A sophisticated and realistic legal framework for regulation of the markets is still in developmental stages. On the one hand, there are simply too many rules and regulations, which were formed without a basis. On the other hand, those regulations that *do* exist are not, in effect, properly or uniformly enforced. In surveying the legal and regulatory problems in emerging markets, the following topics are most frequently encountered:

- The quality of companies permitted to list on the stock exchange.
- Exchange regulations and practices which tend to serve the interest of brokers and not the investing community as a whole.
- The lack of government enforcement of regulations and the lack of initiative on the part of the government to make changes in the market structure.

- Settlement and trading difficulties.
- Difficulties with capital repatriation.
- Discrimination against foreigners as regards to share ownership and the establishment of complex security classes for outsiders and locals.

Very often brokers do not obtain the best available bargains for customers. Also, prompt and timely execution suffers in a loose regulatory environment. In addition, many brokers are trading on their own account so that the customers' trades may get short shrift. Insider dealing is rife in many markets and it is not unusual for firms to profit from material insider information. "Front running" is also a practice that is not unusual in many markets where there is no adequate regulation to prohibit such activity.

Probably one of the biggest problems facing foreign investors in the emerging markets is the limit of the amount of stock foreigners may purchase in some markets. In Thailand for example, foreign investors often reach their investment limit, and, as a result, pricing of "foreign-registered" shares begins to rise to a premium. A separate "alien board" was established in the market to trade shares. However, the lack of liquidity in many of the foreign alien board shares results in very volatile prices and also opens foreign investors to the risks of market manipulation. Interestingly, the purpose of reserving a limited percentage of shares to foreign investors in some cases was defeated since local investors speculate on the "foreign premium" of shares listed on the alien board. In Korea the 10 percent limit for stock market purchases by foreigners has created severe restrictions for market entry. It also, of course, limits liquidity for local investors as well.

Thailand's Proposal to Permit Foreign Investors

In some cases, rules regarding the amount that prices may move within a certain trading period results in excessive market manipulation and often high volatility, exactly what the rule is expected to limit. By having such a restriction, it is often easy for market manipulators to push prices up to the limit price with very small trades and thus give the appearance of rapidly rising or rapidly falling share prices.

When Thailand proposed in late 1992 to allow foreigners to invest legally in Thai stocks without being restricted by foreign ownership limits, the premium prices that investors had had to pay for the limited number of foreign-designated shares fell dramatically and caused significant paper losses for some investors. For many years, foreign demand for blue-chip Thai companies has outstripped supplies. In addition to sometimes purchasing shares at a premium, other foreigners try to circumvent the limits by purchasing local shares through Thai nominees. This was an illegal practice but the authorities did not take action to stop it for fear of driving away investors. However, in its move toward modernization, the stock exchange of Thailand opened its securities depository center in September 1992, thus replacing physical delivery of scrips with computerized account balancing with the shares held at the center. Foreign investors not registered in their own names therefore lost dividends and other entitlements such as rights shares. The new Securities Deposit Center System demands full disclosure at book closing time of the ultimate beneficiaries of bonus issues and dividends. But then the Deputy Secretary General of the Thai Securities and Exchange Commission said that he would allow continuing foreign involvement in local shares and went so far as saying that the law would not be enforced. This did not satisfy local custodial banks acting on behalf of foreigners who refused to continue acting as nominees' fronts. The Thais have sought to allay foreigners' fears and overcome those problems by proposing the establishment of trusts similar to those used in Mexico. These trusts would hold the many shares bought by foreigners and perform the service of dividend collection and other entitlements such as bonus shares. Foreigners could thus legally buy more and more liquid local shares at local market prices, sacrificing only voting rights.

Reforms in the Israeli Securities Market

One example of the changes that take place in various emerging markets securities systems can be found in Israel. After the collapse of the Israeli market in 1983, there were far-reaching reforms in the securities market. When the market collapsed, trading in the stock exchanges was suspended for two weeks until the government entered with a massive bailout. Over the following years monetary policy was liberalized and steps were taken to relax foreign currency limitations while the government embarked on a program to reduce direct intervention in the capital market. A public commission which had examined what had gone wrong in 1983 blamed the securities authority for surrendering to the demands of both internal and external pressure groups, thus leaving the public defenseless. In its 20 years of existence the securities authority had filed only two indictments for alleged violations. The new regulations began requiring quarterly rather than semi-annual financial reports, and recommended establishing independent accounting boards modeled after the U.S. Financial Standards Accounting Board. Most important of all were innovations where the securities authority was able to finance class action lawsuits initiated by minority shareholders as well as equalizing the voting rights of shares issued by public corporations. Previously managers could put up 10 percent of the equity of the firm and gain complete control.

Rivalries and Lack of Unity

Unfortunately, many stock exchanges around the world are operated by the brokerage communities only, with little regard for the other participants in the market such as listed companies, small shareholders, institutional shareholders, and the general public. One good example is the two Philippine stock exchanges, the Manila and the Makati Stock Exchanges. Over the years, the difficulty of getting those two exchanges to merge was an indication of the problems of embedded interest groups. The difficulties of Rosario Lopez, the chairperson of the Securities and Exchange Commission of the Philippines, in her attempts to to merge the two markets is instructive. When she became the chairperson of the Philippines' SEC in 1989, Mrs. Lopez argued that a single exchange would simplify listing procedures, strengthen enforcement of regulations, and eliminate arbitrage between the two exchanges so that market manipulation could be minimized. But the rivalry between the two exchanges was difficult to rectify. The Manila Stock Exchange was established in 1927, making it one of Asia's oldest exchanges. The Makati Stock Exchange had only been established in 1963 when some brokers from the Manila Stock Exchange left to establish a rival stock exchange, which charged lower commission rates, in the new Manila suburb of Makati. The unification started to progress only after President Ramos of the Philippines intervened and gave them until the end of 1992 to unify.

Risks in emerging markets should not overwhelm the investors, since risks must be weighed against the potential returns. Three people in different walks of life made the following pertinent statements:

If I haven't made any errors, that means I haven't made any decisions.—*A Philosopher*

Those who do nothing are never wrong.—*Unknown*

The greatest right in the world is the right to be wrong.—*William Randolph Hearst.*

Chapter Seven

Investment Strategies and Techniques

INVESTMENT PRINCIPLES

S trategies and techniques for successful investing are many and varied. However, over the years as investment management has become the subject of more and more study, a number of principles have emerged (from such renowned investors as Sir John Templeton), which have particular relevance and provide useful guidelines for the investor in emerging markets. Scientific confirmation of the viability of these principles has yet to be made, though anecdotal evidence suggests that they have stood the test of time and have been successfully applied.

Hard Work and Discipline

Someone asked me once if I could condense the most important qualities needed for a good investor into three words and I replied, "Motivation, hard work, and discipline." At one time Vidal Sassoon remarked, "The only place where success comes before work is in the dictionary." It stands to reason that the more time and effort put into researching investments, the more knowledge will be gained and wiser decisions will be made. Sir John Templeton has pointed out that a good deal of humility is also required: "The investor who has all the answers doesn't even understand the questions."

Several well-known personalities substantiate the above quotations, as follows:

Genius is 1 percent inspiration and 99 percent perspiration.

—*Thomas A. Edison*

The harder you work the luckier you get.—*Gary Player (golf pro)*
It takes 20 years to make an overnight success.
                                        —Eddie Cantor (comedy star)

Common Sense

Napoleon is quoted as having said, "In any undertaking, two-thirds depends on reason, one-third on chance. Increase the first fraction and you are fainthearted. Increase the second and you are foolhardy." I like to think that common sense is most important when making investment decisions since the words *common sense* imply the clarity and simplification required to integrate successfully all the complex information with which investors are faced.

Creativity

A significant amount of creativity is required for successful investing since it is necessary to look at investments from a multi-faceted approach considering all the variables that could negatively or positively affect an investment. Also, creative thinking is required to look forward to the future and forecast the outcome of current business plans.

Two adages that also state the importance of creativity are:

Imagination is more important than knowledge.—*Albert Einstein*
The best way to have a good idea is to have many ideas.
                                        —Linus Pauling

Diversification

Sir John Templeton once said, "To avoid having all your eggs in the wrong basket at the wrong time, every investor should diversify." Diversification as depicted here is particularly important in emerging markets where individual country or company risks can be extreme. For this reason global investing is always superior to investing on only the investor's home market or one market. If you search worldwide, you will find more bargains and better bargains than by studying only one nation.

Independence

A number of successful investors have commented on the importance of independence and individual decision making. When making investments, it is most unlikely that committee decisions can be superior to a well thought-out individual decision. This might be a good place to recall several pertinent quotations.

> A committee is a gathering of important people who singly can do nothing but together can decide that nothing can be done.—*Unknown*
>
> If you buy the same securities as other people, you will have the same results as other people . . . When any method for selecting stocks becomes popular then switch to unpopular methods . . . Too many investors can spoil any share-selection method or any market-timing formula . . . It is impossible to produce a superior performance unless you do something different from the majority . . . To buy when others are despondently selling and to sell when others are greedily buying requires the greatest fortitude and pays the greatest rewards . . . The best performance is produced by a person, not a committee.
>
> *—Sir John Templeton*
>
> A committee is a group of people who keep minutes and waste hours.—*Unknown*
>
> Nothing is ever accomplished by a committee unless it is made up of three persons, one of whom is sick and another absent.—*Unknown*
>
> Only dead fish swim with the current.—*Unknown*
>
> To be great is to be misunderstood.—*Ralph Waldo Emerson*.

Risk-Taking

Peter Drucker once said, "In every success story, you find someone has made a courageous decision." Investment decisions always require decisions based on insufficient information. There is never enough time to learn all there is to know about an investment and even if there were, equity investments are like living organisms undergoing continuous change. There always comes the time when a decision must be taken and a risk acquired. The ability to take that risk based on the best diligently gathered available information is the mark of a good investor and, I might add, a good businessperson.

Value Orientation

The emphasis on value in investing is not universally accepted and when accepted often not applied. Sir John Templeton has said that there is a tendency for too many investors to focus on "outlook" or "trend." Therefore, more opportunities may be uncovered by focusing on value. Studies have shown that over the long term, stock market prices tend to be influenced by the asset value and earnings capabilities of listed shares. Also, share prices tend to fluctuate much more widely then values. Therefore it is unlikely that index funds will ever produce the best total return performance. The value approach to investing was first and best defined by Benjamin Graham and David Dodd in their 1934 book *Security Analysis*. In the book, they articulated the system of buying "value" shares whose price is relative to such factors as earnings, dividends, or book assets. Studies have been made showing that value investing in a number of countries will work over the long term. But studies have also revealed conflicting conclusions regarding its application. For example, one study showed that investing in shares with a low ratio of share price to cash flow was a better strategy than buying shares with a low price-to-book ratio. Others indicate that price-earnings ratios are the best determinate of future prices. Accounting standards differ from one country to another, so that treatment of accounting items varies significantly. These differences result not only from historical precedent but also because of changing taxation policies. Of course, the differences of accounting standards are not exclusive to the emerging markets. Since accounts do not tell the whole story, it is important to meet management face to face and to ensure that the company's operations are also inspected. Attention to detail is important. Again, we quote two people:

> A handful of men have become very rich by paying attention to details that most others ignored.—*Henry Ford*
>
> It has long been an axiom of mine that the little things are definitely the most important.—*Sir Arthur Conan Doyle*

Flexibility

It is important for investors to be flexible and not permanently adopt a particular type of asset or selection method. The best approach is to migrate from the popular to the unpopular securities, sectors, or methods.

Timing and Staying Invested

Investors often ask: "When should I invest in the market?" The most insightful answer provided by Sir John Templeton is: "The best time to invest is when you have money." What this means is that equity investing is the best way to preserve value rather than leaving money in a bank account. A corollary to this principle is that investment should not be sold unless a much better investment has been found to replace it.

The Long-Term View

I know that it is very difficult to reply to investors who expect fast gains and even more difficult when they invest in a fund and almost immediately see the net asset value turn sour. That's why I advise representatives from the very start of their sales process to underline to their clients and repeat the importance of long-term investing and dollar averaging. We, as investment managers, have a policy of looking to the long term because experience has shown us that if we try to make short-term gains the results will work against outstanding performance. Since most investors look at the short term, then we certainly should not do that. By looking at the long-term growth and prospects of companies and countries, particularly those stocks that are out of favor or unpopular, the chances of obtaining a superior return are much greater.

Investment Averaging

Another point that should be remembered by investors is the importance of investment averaging by purchasing consistently in a measured and periodic pattern. When the Templeton Emerging Markets Fund started in early 1987, it experienced a disastrous performance that first year with the loss in value of the Fund in excess of 20 percent. However, those investors who purchased more shares at lower prices went on to reap greater rewards. Investors who establish a program from the very beginning to purchase shares over a set period of intervals have the opportunity to purchase at not only high prices, but also low prices, bringing their average cost down.

Accepting Market Cycles

Any study of stock markets around the world will show that bear or bull markets have always been temporary. It is clear that markets do have cyclical behavior with pessimistic, sceptical, optimistic, euphoric, panic, and depressive phases. Investors should thus expect such variations and plan accordingly. Sir John Templeton stated: "The time of maximum pessimism is the best time to buy, and the time of maximum optimism is the best time to sell. If you can see the light at the end of the tunnel then it is probably already too late to buy." According to one study of investment managers, historical performance, often the primary consideration in most investment manager selection decisions, was found to be a useless random statistic. Another study showed the absence of any predictive value in historical performance rankings of money managers. That research indicated that the characteristics most helpful in identifying managers who achieve superior, long-term results included the following:

1. *Independent thinking.* Independent evaluation of available information and adopting non-consensus views.
2. *Unencumbered decision making.* Avoidance of complex, time-consuming hierarchical information flows and committee decisions.
3. *Discipline.* Best managers are highly focused, intense, and enthusiastic.
4. *Flexibility.* Portfolio management requires commitment to change. A manager must always be willing to reverse his or her earlier decision regardless of whether it was good or bad without the slightest hesitation.
5. *Passion for investing.* Successful managers love what they do and see it as a personal passion.

There is a continuing controversy and discussion regarding the best way to manage an emerging markets portfolio or, for that matter, any equity portfolio. The subject is fraught with dangers, simply because definitions and categorization of investment styles tend to pigeon hole a particular style and lead to extreme simplification. For example, some investment managers are categorized as "top-down." According to this simplistic notion, a top-down manager will first select, which countries he would like to invest in through a pre-analysis of the economic and political environment and then, at the second stage, take individual stocks within those markets, often based on liquidity and market capitalization considerations, enabling the manager to enter and exit the market easily.

The other categorization used is the "bottom-up" manager who pays most attention to finding the best companies globally in all emerging markets, ignoring the country allocation decision entirely and focusing on company information rather than macroeconomic and macropolitical data.

Of course, these categorizations of bottom-up and top-down are gross simplifications and it is difficult to find managers who neatly fit those descriptions. More often than not, some managers would tend to emphasize stock selection whereas others would tend to emphasize country allocation but both would at all times be considering macroeconomic and macropolitical as well as individual stock differences. It is difficult for any managers to ignore the following:

- Matters regarding earnings.
- Growth and momentum of companies.
- The evaluation of companies.
- Interest rates and their impact on alternatives facing investors in a particular market.
- Liquidity of the market.
- Market capitalization of companies (particularly as emerging market funds grow and require larger single investments to make a significant impact on portfolios).
- Economic policies of the country.
- The political environment and market-related factors such as investor sentiments and market rumors.

One of the more interesting aspects of emerging markets is the wide variety of influences impacting on market behavior. Moreover, these influences are changing from day to day, providing excellent opportunities for investors to discern times when markets are overvalued or undervalued.

More and more work is now being done on computerized models for country allocations and other selection requirements. As data regarding emerging markets becomes more available and as historical series are built up, such computerized techniques will become more important in emerging markets investment programs. Already models offering trade-offs of risk and return models are available and being used. In one model, for example, selections of which markets in which to place the largest portion of the assets are allocated to those with a most favorable combination of historically high returns, low volatility, and low correlation with other markets. Unfortunately, many of these models rely on historical data.

RESEARCHING EMERGING MARKETS

An analyst or portfolio manager must constantly be aware of the influences and biases affecting him. These influences and biases are strongest in the places where one spends most of his or her working and leisure hours and from where a person obtains most information. For this reason the emerging markets analysts must continually visit all the countries in the emerging markets areas *and* read news and research reports originating from all over the world.

Is it important to obtain data from advisers and analysts based in the country in which the investments are being made? Can such an approach result in the best portfolio returns? Experience has shown us that total reliance on a locally based analyst or adviser is not sufficient and will eventually tend to lead toward returns inferior to that of a more comprehensive approach. Thomas Jefferson said: "The correct behavior for advisers is to question everything, produce nothing, and talk at the right time." Someone else remarked, "Advisers are people who borrow your watch, tell you the time, and then don't give it back." For wise portfolio decisions, two important perspectives are necessary:

1. The global outlook and experience that comes from having invested in many countries.

2. The more detailed and intimate knowledge that comes from a
   local presence.

It is important to combine both perspectives by having local and
country-specific information collated, digested, and compared
with other global data. This kind of analysis yields much more
powerful results, which enhance the locally gathered information
by, for example, providing insights into a particular company as a
consequence of comparisons with similar companies in another
country. The end results are much more valuable insights that
must yield far better long-term investment returns.

Of course, the local information is best gathered by informants
who are living in the particular country and who have an intimate
knowledge of the local environment. However, we have found
that this cannot replace the frequent visits the analyst makes to
each country in which investments are made, since we have found
that local analysts need assistance and support in knowing which
questions to ask. More importantly, the combination of local and
foreign analysts leads to much more valuable insights. Analysts
based in the country that they are analyzing will often overlook
very vital points of inquiry because they have been blinded by close
interaction with the local management or other members of the
community. Someone visiting from abroad is able to introduce an
entirely different perspective and raise new and unique questions,
which could throw an entirely different light on the subject matter.

Recently, while I was in Istanbul interviewing executives at a
copper mining company, I noticed that our local consultant's questions centered around the firm's mining techniques and
efficiencies. Accompanying us was one of our analysts who had
studied similar mining companies. He entered into an entirely new
line of questioning when he asked whether this Turkish company
was able to achieve profit margins above similar mining companies
in the Philippines and Chile. He wondered whether it was because
of the company's investments in copper futures and currency
trading profits. This question opened up an altogether different
framework and enabled us to lead the company's executives into a
hitherto ignored but important facet of this firm's operations.
Thus we revised our entir assessment of the company and its
prospects.

Can an analyst be overinfluenced by local factors and thus be better off assessing investments from a distance? Yes, analysts may be overinfluenced by local factors, but globalists and generalists may also miss the important local details, particularly if a bottom-up style of investing is used. I have found that the best remedy for too local a view or too global a view is by combining and synthesizing both. Good portfolio management requires a blend of all relevant information in order to achieve the best results. The best approach is to obtain the most detailed and accurate information, which can only come from local analysts aided and abetted by global analysts, and then digest that data from a global perspective.

Clients often feel more comfortable with an analyst or manager who is on-site and living in the area in which the investing takes place. Investors are often impressed when meeting local experts, and well they should be since such local experts provide invaluable information. However, sole reliance on such information can be dangerous without a global perspective. We have found that a heavy local bias can eventually lead to severe misinterpretations and give rise to unwise investment decisions. When the Indonesian market was booming in 1989 and 1990, it was very difficult to find local analysts able to admit the severe over-valuation in that market. They all seemed to feel that the rapidly rising market would continue indefinitely. Those outside the country, however, could perceive the clear and present danger and thus refrained from aggressive buying. As much as 50 percent of one Indonesian fund was kept in cash despite strong protestations from clients wishing us to catch the bull run. The subsequent disastrous fall in the market vindicated one fund manager's value approach but it is highly unlikely that he could have taken that stance if he had been caught up in the local feeding frenzy. An outside perspective, at that time, was invaluable and subsequently resulted in outperformance of the fund.

COMPANY ANALYSIS

In emerging markets, we are constantly reminded of the need for independent research and careful checking what company officials and underwriters tell us. To paraphrase that great film pioneer Samuel Goldwyn: "A verbal promise isn't worth the paper it is written on."

One of the key aspects of investing in emerging markets is the need to perform a careful analysis of companies. Normally, the further back in time the analysis goes, the better. Such factors as a sound balance sheet, high return on equity, strong self-financing capability, good profit margins, and good profit growth are some of the items sought when analysis is undertaken. This sort of analysis requires the fund manager to have a reliable and timely access to audited accounts. This presents many problems since each country has different accounting standards. Improperly or falsely presented materials can mislead a fund manager into buying a stock that he normally would not purchase. Characteristically, there is only a limited amount of information available on emerging markets. In some countries companies listed on the stock exchange and companies planning initial public offerings, rights issues, or privatization offers do not offer the public timely, informative, and detailed financial statements. In a number of emerging markets, there are no requirements and enforcement in this regard. There is often a lack of control regarding when or how financial information is released or distributed so that it will be accessible not only to major investors but also to the general public.

In the past, these problems have been compounded by the lack of incentive for many emerging market companies to reveal information regarding their operations. They are often closely controlled corporations, dominated by founding families or their heirs, where the majority of shares are held by family members. Their public listing is often made to obtain tax benefits and not to raise additional capital. Trading, settlement, and regulatory systems are also evolving and differ between individual markets as well as from the standards typical in the developed world.

To meet this challenge, painstaking research is required, involving on-the-spot analysis and extensive traveling. This involves examining individual shares on a five-year or longer view, paying particular attention to the potential for, and the stability of, earnings growth.

The Use of Ratio Analysis

There are many ways to appraise financial statements, but one of the most common is the use of ratio analysis whereby the various elements in financial statements are compared. When looking at the value of a firm, such ratios as price/earnings, dividend yield percentage, return on equity, and price/book value are used. When assessing profitability, such ratios as profit margins, return on equity, return on assets are used. When assessing safety or balance sheet strength, such ratios as debt-to-equity and current ratio are used. There are severe limitations on using only one ratio or relying too heavily on one type of analysis. For example, when analyzing banks, the capital adequacy ratio is often cited as an important factor when considering their viability. However, the capital adequacy ratio as stated by the Bank for International Settlements only takes into account credit risks and excludes market risks that the banks are exposed to in their trading and investment portfolios in foreign currency, share, and money markets.

Trends in movements of funds and changes in various categories in the balance sheet are often the focus of attention by analysts. Trends such as percentage changes in sales, assets, liabilities, and cash flow can be revealing to the analyst.

The Importance of Detailed and Local Data

Detailed and accurate local information is important because without such information, a generalist's interpretation can be severely warped and lead to equally unwise investment decisions. It is for this reason that significant resources should be placed on obtaining the best and most specific local information possible. Individual companies are carefully studied and visited so that when that data is eventually placed in a global databank it can assist in finding the world's best investment bargains. Without this attention to local detail and accuracy, a global analytical approach is useless. Fortunately, in this world of rapid and efficient telecommunications, data reaching us is more timely and comprehensive than ever before. In addition, the more convenient travel arrangements now possible enable us to make more frequent on-site visits which adds to the store of experience and knowledge so vital to perceptive investment decisions.

STATISTICS

There are three kinds of lies: lies, damned lies, and statistics.—
Benjamin Disraeli

If all economists were laid end to end, they still would not reach a
conclusion.—*George Bernard Shaw*

A controversy over the real state of Poland's trade in 1992 underlined the problems of making economic decisions on the basis of doubtful and often contradictory statistics. Questions were raised in March 1993 when Poland's Foreign Trade Ministry issued figures, based on customs data, which pointed to a $2.5 billion deficit in 1992. These contradicted earlier figures, collated by the National Bank and seized on by the government as proof of Poland's strong economic performance, which showed a surplus of $512 million.

The Fudging of Statistics

In countries accustomed to fudging statistics, we see many disagreements over data between various government agencies. For example, in August 1992 the Ministry of International Economic Relations (MIER) and the National Bank of Hungary (NBH) all published sharply contrasting figures. The MIER said that the country's trade deficit in the first half of the year was $800 million while the NBH said it was about $100 million.

Underground economic activities in many countries inhibit the accurate gathering of statistics. For example, official estimates put the number of informal workers in downtown Rio de Janeiro at more than 300,000. In the whole country, there are at least 28 million people obtaining their daily income from the underground economy, according to some economists.

Fund managers know that when purchasing millions of dollars worth of shares around the world on a daily basis, information regarding pricing is essential. This information must be timely and available while trading on the stock exchange floor is transacted, or at least immediately after the close of trading. Fund management companies subscribe to a number of very expensive, electronic stock price information systems such as Reuters. However, many emerging markets are not sufficiently covered by these services or even not covered at all. In some cases, this is because the host country stock exchange restricts the release of such information to independent information services. This is, of course, a severe impediment. Emerging stock markets should freely make available such information and even subsidize its dissemination worldwide since this will popularize their market and increase trading turnover.

High inflation and extreme currency fluctuations create a range of unique problems for emerging market analysts. For example, in high-inflation economies such as Brazil and Argentina, accounts need frequent adjustment for inflation. These adjustments require an entire set of rules that may differ from one country to another. Adding to extreme currency fluctuations, it can be seen why corporate comparisons become a time-consuming and difficult process.

The risk of oversimplification when looking at emerging market economies is very great. It is easy to think of countries as economic units. In fact, most countries are not homogeneous and a conclusion drawn about a country as a whole is often wrong.

Weakness in income growth may mask real changes in welfare for large parts of the poor population. Improvements in meeting the basic needs for food, education, health care, equality of opportunity, civil liberties, and environmental protection are not captured by statistics on income growth, for example.

In February 1993, a former Soviet Prime Minister, Valentin S. Pavlov, boasted that he had been able to fool foreign bankers into believing that the Soviet Union possessed ample gold reserves. He is reported as saying: "We used to attract a huge amount of private banking capital. They brought us their money as if we were a savings bank." He said that the Soviet Union had squandered its gold reserves long before commonly supposed but concealed the fact in order to attract Western loans.

INFORMATION SOURCES

The best sources of information are company staff members, the staff of competitors, the audited financial statements, and professional experts in various fields. There are also a number of brokerage houses with excellent research facilities. If used correctly, such facilities can provide rich source data. With more and more brokers involved in merchant banking and taking positions on their own behalf, caution is required since there is a tendency for brokers to put forward information in order to promote a particular stock in which they may have a vested interest. Furthermore, if a broker is distributing a glossy publication to hundreds of investors, then chances of it being a bargain are lower by the time investors read it. In 1991, one major New York brokerage house reported the largest profit share came from trading *on its own behalf and "market making"* rather than broking. Investors must therefore be aware of broker recommendations since those recommendations may be biased in favor of the brokers' own accounts. In addition, analyses must be carefully checked against audited financial statements since definitions of various accounting ratios may differ significantly.

The Importance of Detailed and Intensive Research

Many investors have found that the best approach is based on fundamental value-oriented research. However, in applying such an investment philosophy to emerging markets, modifications are required. Since the universe of emerging markets is focused and more limited than a global portfolio, analysis must be more flexible in the selection of criteria when evaluating companies. Criteria must differ between countries and industries. For example, the use of book value as a criteria may be flawed in some markets because of some idiosyncrasy of the accounting methods used in that country, while in other markets it could be an excellent measure of value.

Detailed and intensive research is critical in emerging markets. In the first instance the analyst must focus on essential company performance characteristics unfiltered through macro-political and macro-economic lenses. Emerging market countries tend to be perceived as subject to wide swings in political and economic activity. This tends to influence and perhaps distort the investor's perception of the individual company investment. Those political and economic factors should not influence evaluations of the viability of an individual company investment except if they have a direct bearing on the company's viability to operate and produce profits over the long term.

Starting with this individual company focus places great demands on the information-gathering and analytical skills of the investor. Emerging markets tend to have a shortage of adequate detailed company information gathered in a consistent way over a long historical time span. The task of obtaining such information is often enormous in countries where regulations regarding company disclosure are inadequate (or inadequately enforced) and where public companies are often considered the private domain of the owners or their families. An information request from a minority stockholder in some cases is considered presumptuous. It is in such environments that good local contacts and sources of information are essential so that the required information may be obtained. It is thus of great importance for the investment organization to have a long history of local relationships.

There must be an ability and willingness for the emerging markets researcher to obtain information from all relevant sources, whether it be local or international. In other words, total reliance cannot be placed on just local information or on only foreign information. Both have relevance and value because of the varying perspectives they present. Also, the combination of (a) a local consultant or analyst living in the country, (b) a foreign-based analyst focusing on that particular country, and (c) a global expert capable of analyzing a particular industry or sector, offers the best coalition for effective portfolio management. Finally, the investment team must try their best to exercise a great deal of objectivity in their analysis of all the relevant data so that local or foreign, or company-specific or industry-specific, data may be given appropriate weighting.

ACCOUNTING IN EMERGING MARKETS

Company-audited accounts are necessarily the starting place for examination of any company in the emerging markets. Audited financial statements provide the first source of information an analyst has about a particular company. These statements are supposed to show an unbiased account of the company's health and business. As for the demands on the analytical skills of the investor in evaluating those emerging market companies, most daunting are the varying accounting standards used in each country and, more importantly, the varying taxation regimes which impinge on how accounting standards are applied. It is essential, therefore, for the analyst to ensure that he or she understands what methods the firm's management and its accountants are using in their efforts to minimize their tax liability. In addition, the high inflation and currency devaluations in many emerging market countries influence the accuracy of accounts since various (and differing) methods of inflation adjustments, decreed either by the accounting standards organizations or by the government, could render accounts all but meaningless for the value investor examining the long-term growth prospects of a company. Despite efforts on the part of various accounting organizations around the world to come together and agree on some basic standards, the differences between countries are enormous, not necessarily because of a lack of agreement regarding how accounts should be handled, but because of local laws and regulations that impose certain requirements different from what would be normally considered "generally accepted accounting practices." However, even in the developed markets the very detailed rules and disclosure requirements are often viewed as a burden rather than as a boon to accountants. One accountant said, "I am a certified public accountant, but every time I read a pension footnote I have to refresh my understanding of what the various data mean. This is also true of the income tax information."

Regulatory officials around the world are deeply divided regarding such questions as what accounting standards should be required. The fact that accounting firms are consistently being sued by shareholders for large amounts indicates the degree of dispute regarding accounting standards and applications.

Accounting Differences between Countries and Regions

Differences of accounting between countries and regions have been with us for quite some time. For example, many emerging countries influenced by continental European accounting practices have a uniform chart of accounts. In countries influenced by British and American accounting, the chart of accounts is more flexible and, while not using an established format, tend to have more extensive information in the notes of the accounts. In continental European accounts, there is greater use of legal reserves and tax-based reserves, whereas in the United States the emphasis is on the concept of *fair presentation* and excessive arbitrary reserves are uncommon. In some countries, the process of accounting is very much the subject of government regulation whereas in others, the main influence comes from accountancy bodies.

Since auditor selection is determined by the company's management or directors, biases in the accounts may occur. In one case a company in China hired a major foreign accounting firm to audit its accounts. However, when the accounts were qualified by that accounting firm, a new firm was appointed! With increasing lawsuits brought by investors against auditors, auditors are now being much more careful regarding which accounts they will accept and then, after the audit work is granted and accepted, they will look carefully to ensure that the audit was done as objectively as possible.

Accounting in China

China is perhaps the best example of how change is taking place in emerging market accounting. Currently much of the accounting is still done without the use of computers and accounting varies from one area of the country to another. However, gradually government rules are changing to correct various discrepancies and computers are being introduced to speed up the process. One sign of the need for better accounting was recognized when a major international accounting firm won a U.S.$2.6 million contract to develop accounting standards for China, awarded by the Chinese Ministry of Finance. The object of the World Bank-financed contract was to bring accounting and auditing practices in China into harmony with international standards. In China, as in other parts of the emerging world, the major accounting firms have established offices or joint ventures. Many of the "Big Six" have expanded rapidly and are training accountants in order to meet the ever-increasing demand.

In Brazil, the complications of inflation accounting and rapid changes in tax applications for accountants create substantial problems. For example, in 1993 many companies challenged in the Brazilian courts the validity of certain tax and regulatory changes decreed in prior years, which dealt with restatements of accounts, tax credits, and social contribution provisions. Many companies received favorable decisions in the court and thus could defy regulatory changes.

In countries where inflation is very high, such as Brazil, monetary restatement of financial statements in line with inflation has become mandatory. Starting in 1987, for example, all Brazilian companies were required to restate their financial statements in line with price indexes. Even before that time, revaluations of property, plant, and equipment were authorized within certain limits in 1944, 1951, and 1956. In the system, permanent assets or non-monetary assets or liabilities were linked to an index so that they could be stated in current purchasing power in financial statements, thus resulting in a continuing revaluation of assets as inflation moves forward.

One example of the degree to which revisions can affect accounts for emerging market companies, particularly those in countries emerging from Socialist economies, can be seen in work required to revise and assess the accounts of one Chinese company listed on the New York Stock Exchange at the end of 1992. According to the underwriters, the accounting work took up 11,000 labor-hours of expert accountants with accounts for the past three years restated in line with American standards. A team of 20 experts from the accounting firm had to spend two months in China to complete the work.

Distorted Accounts

A number of variations and accounting innovations can result in distorted accounts. In one case, a bus company established a "fuel price equalization account" and showed it on the balance sheet as a current liability which acted to smooth earnings results. At the beginning of each year a *standard fuel price* (SFP) based on historical prices was determined. If the actual fuel price was below the SFP, a fuel equalization reserve equal to the difference between the standard fuel price and the actual cost of fuel was charged against the profit and loss statement and transferred to the fuel price equalization account, thus giving the appearance of lower company earnings. If the actual fuel price was higher than the standard fuel price, a fuel equalization reserve was released from that equalization account and credited to the profit and loss account, thus helping to raise earnings.

An Example of Misleading Accounting

One example of misleading accounting and insider dealing occurred in a Hong Kong company. The major shareholders knew that the financial conditions of their major customer in the United States had deteriorated. They therefore quietly sold their shares on the market. The share price was driven down from $2.40 in 1988 to $0.23 in 1989. However, in an announcement on April 27, 1989, the directors stated, "The Directors of the Company have noted the recent decrease in the price of the Company's shares although the Company is not aware of any reason for such decreases. . . ." On May 5, 1989, the company made another announcement: ". . . The Company's U.S. customer announced on April 17, 1989, that it was carrying out a reorganization plan regarding its corporate structure. The Company does not believe that this will have any effect on its operations." On May 24, 1989, another company announcement said, "The chairman of the Company has informed the Board of the Company that his holding in the Company has been substantially reduced by sales in the open market throughout the last five months up to the present time and that he no longer has a significant shareholding in the company." The listing of the Company was suspended by the Stock Exchange of Hong Kong that same day. In actuality, unannounced by the directors, the company started to have losses in September 1989 and continued to have losses through to the end of the year. Meanwhile the chairman started selling in November and continued until he had disposed of 99 percent of his holdings by May 1990.

By speeding up the sale of his shares between March and May of 1989, the chairman aimed to avoid a fall in the firm's share price once the 1988 results were published. He was reported to have pocketed nearly $112 million from the share sales and saved himself at least $22 million as the share price slipped down from $1.10 in February 1989 to $0.55 by May. Once the extent of his disposal became known, the shares collapsed to $0.24 in June and prompted minority shareholders to force his resignation from the company.

Different Terms Used in Different Ways Worldwide

Care must be taken when interpreting accounting terms since different terms are used in different ways by accountants around the world. The words may be in English but the meanings could differ substantially. In Sri Lanka, one set of accounts used the term *fictitious assets* to describe what in actuality were prepayments. In one case in China a firm used a term in the accounts which was translated by the Hong Kong Chinese as *pension fund liabilities*. In fact, the Chinese characters used by the mainland Chinese had a different meaning from that assumed by the Hong Kong Chinese. Actually the meaning was not *pension fund liabilities* but *development reserves*. This difference in translation made a significant impact on analysis of the firm's balance sheet, since in one case the item was a liability while in the other case an asset (and a very significant one, at that).

Even in Europe harmonization of financial reporting has a long way to go. Anglo-Saxon accounting systems tend to be more oriented toward shareholders and focus on disclosure, whereas continental accounts are rooted in Roman law and are more oriented toward creditors, guided by government rules and dominated by tax requirements. The International Accounting Standards Committee has embarked on a simplification program to reduce the number of options it judges acceptable in its standards.

Many companies and countries are resistant to change but with the globalization of emerging markets and as companies seek funding and capital from outside their own country, they will feel the need to change their accounting systems. In the end, a lot will depend on the integrity and standards set by the international accounting profession. It appears that gradually under the threat of lawsuits on the part of disgruntled shareholders and the need to preserve their reputations, many international accountants are now resigning from assignments or avoiding firms which they deem do not meet their standards.

Disclosure of Financial Information

The main factors influencing disclosure of financial information in companies is the pattern of ownership and the scope of company operations. According to studies done by the Center for International Financial Analysis and Research, Inc., companies that have shareholders in more than one country or whose operations go beyond domestic borders, tend to have greater disclosure regarding their company's operations since they must cater to international investors. Multinational corporations thus have higher disclosure than purely domestic companies. In addition, companies that are closely controlled, or whose majority shareholders have a large proportion of shares, tend to be less forthcoming in their disclosure.

Banks and financial organizations tend to have less disclosure compared with other companies such as industrial companies or insurance companies. One of the reasons for this is that most of the major banks are closely regulated and thus have neither the incentive nor the inclination to disclose more than what is required by the law.

Common Accounting Practices

Differences in accounting practices are great and too numerous to mention but some of the more common ones include:

1. *Tax treatment.* Each country has a different tax regime and within countries different industries and geographical areas may have varying tax requirements. Accountants will, of

course, attempt to minimize taxes by their accounts presentation.

2. *Off-balance-sheet items*. The use of off-balance-sheet items could be rather significant in a number of countries. For example, the balance sheets of companies in some countries may not reveal financing where controlled associated companies are not consolidated.

3. *Treatment of intangibles*. In some countries, such items as goodwill can be capitalized whereas in other countries they are not. For example, goodwill arising from company mergers is inconsistently treated around the world. Some countries allow the reduction of goodwill directly from shareholders' equity whereas others require it to be amortized over varying time spans.

4. *Reserves*. There are different treatments for reserves and in some countries reserves are provided so that management can smooth results between years. Discretionary or general reserves are allowed in some countries and not in others. These reserves are related to the revaluation of fixed assets. Earnings may be reduced or increased by management decisions regarding the adjustment of these reserves. Net income may thus be distorted, making it difficult to evaluate the performance of companies. Hidden reserves are often allowed for banks by some countries. As a result, earnings are distorted and there is great allowance for management to adjust reserves and distort income.

5. *Currency exchange*. The exchange rates used (and when they are used) differ from country to country and thus have a significant influence on accounts. Companies around the world differ in the foreign currency translation methods used and sometimes the gains or losses from transactions are not clearly segregated.

6. *Valuation of assets or inventory*. Some countries allow periodic revaluation of assets whereas others do not. Marketable securities often are given a different value so that in some cases they are given at cost or in other cases at market value. Different methods are used to value inventory, some at cost and some at realizable value, some at replacement costs and other methods.

7. *Depreciation*. This is one of the more common cost items which is used differently from one country to another. In

some cases, governments give specific guidelines for depreciation timetables. In one country, an asset may be depreciated over 10 years and in another country the same asset might be depreciated over 30 years. It is therefore difficult to compare such accounting items as the cost of goods sold, fixed assets, retained earnings, and deferred income taxes between companies and countries.

8. *Revenue recognition.* The recognition of revenue and the timing of such recognition varies greatly from one country to another. For example, in some countries revenues are recognized when a contract is signed, whereas in other countries they are not recognized until delivery of the goods is made.

9. *Consolidation of subsidiaries.* There is great variation at what point subsidiaries will be consolidated. Although more and more worldwide companies are consolidating subsidiaries where the parent company owns 50 percent or more, there still remain inconsistencies in this practice with some companies consolidating when they own 20 percent of the company and others not until they own more than 50 percent.

10. *Multiple classes of shares.* In many countries there are different classes of shares for a particular company. In Brazil, for example, until recently there were both common and preferred shares and also bearer and registered shares so that there could be four different types of shares for one company.

11. *Inflation accounting.* In high-inflation countries, the treatment of inflation in the accounts varies considerably. More importantly, the inflation rates allowed for application in the accounts varies. In one case in Brazil, for example, the government changed the inflation rate index to be used in accounts, after the accounts were published. For example, in 1991, the government announced that the inflation index they had announced previously for 1990 was incorrect. They then instructed companies to readjust the 1990 accounts for a new index. Then in 1993 the new president, Itamar Franco, decided to revoke the previous 1991 announcement and revert to the original! However, that change was not followed through although it created a market panic when it was announced.

12. *Treatment of losses.* In banks, for example, provisions for loan losses are often treated differently and there are great disparities in the extent to which loan losses are allowed and charged off.

Chapter Eight

The Future of Emerging Markets

The development of emerging equity markets offers the future promise of outstanding benefits for developing the nations' economic growth. Such markets will provide the means whereby these nations may distribute the ownership of privatized companies, provide a method where market forces may allocate financial assets, and most importantly, provide a stimulus for the attraction of new equity capital for growing companies in emerging markets. If these benefits are to be fully realized, the emerging nation governments must create favorable conditions through market liberalization as well as adequate infrastructures (such as computerized trading systems and central depository schemes), which will allow for the smooth operation of efficient equity markets.

There certainly are numerous problems in the world of emerging markets and there are high risks in investing in such nations. But, as someone once said: "Problems are opportunities in work clothes." In emerging markets investment, it is necessary to be optimistic since "the world belongs to optimists; the pessimists are only spectators." However, emerging markets are not the only markets facing numerous problems. The fact remains that there have always been problems and will continue to be so in the coming years throughout the world. But we are entering an era, which is perhaps unparalleled in the history of mankind. With better communications, improved travel, more international commerce, and generally better relations between nations, the opportunities for humanity and for emerging markets investors are better than they have ever been before. With the demise of communism and the coming together of nations around the world, combined with the emergence of China and India as free enterprise market economies, the opportunities for the creation of wealth are unparalleled.

Although some of the stock markets of the developing nations may sometimes seem to be "submerged," they are generally emerging into bigger and better things. The important thing is to keep an open mind and to diversify in global equities. As someone said: "Minds are like parachutes—they only function when they are opened."

Studies have shown that stock market investments made in a patient and consistent manner will invariably grow since there is a natural tendency for equity investments to grow in order to keep up with inflation. In addition, independently managed businesses, competing successfully in the marketplace, are generally winners on the stock markets as there is a tendency for their sales, profits, and assets to expand. However, it is not always possible to predict whether a company is going to be successful or unsuccessful, so it is necessary to diversify. As John Paul Getty remarked, "Money is like fertilizer, you have to spread it around everywhere or it will stink."

One problem facing the world today is the tendency for people to think in shorter and shorter time frames. One recent study indicated that stocks in U.S. companies were held for an average of two years, whereas in the 1960s they used to be held for seven years. Some shareholders look for a quick return on their investments and thus business executives are driven by the same mentality. This short-term philosophy is detrimental to the health of the company and the investor. Unless companies and investors take a longer term view, growth prospects are limited and planning is stunted. Taking a long view of emerging markets will yield excellent results for the investor prepared to be patient and willing to apply sound and tested principles in a diligent and consistent manner.

Index

P. P.   245.   C.   200 210
                                                        9.5   9.75
    Tax. 1.   1.0   190.5 200.25
    Legal   0.9   Mot   144   144
                     1.0   ‾‾‾‾   ‾‾‾‾
                    ‾‾‾‾‾‾   46.5   56.25
                    247.9.
                    183.75
Moty.   ‾‾‾‾‾‾‾   (51.5)
    Dep   64.15
                   ‾‾‾‾‾‾‾

① The Max of 144. @ 7.½ ?
                    40   Bond

② Cash to Close 64k.

③ Int finance 144k.
                   ‾‾‾‾‾‾